A SHORT HISTORY OF LEGAL VALIDITY AND INVALIDITY

A SHORT HISTORY OF LEGAL VALIDITY AND INVALIDITY

Foundations of Private and Public Law

Maris Köpcke

INTERSENTIA

Intersentia Ltd
8 Wellington Street | Cambridge
CB1 1HW | United Kingdom
Tel.: +44 1223 736 170
Email: mail@intersentia.co.uk
www.intersentia.com | www.intersentia.co.uk

Distribution for the UK and Ireland:
NBN International
Airport Business Centre, 10 Thornbury Road
Plymouth, PL6 7PP
United Kingdom
Tel.: +44 1752 202 301 | Fax: +44 1752 202 331
Email: orders@nbninternational.com

Distribution for Europe and all other countries:
Intersentia Publishing nv
Groenstraat 31
2640 Mortsel
Belgium
Tel.: +32 3 680 15 50 | Fax: +32 3 658 71 21
Email: mail@intersentia.be

Distribution for the USA and Canada:
Independent Publishers Group
Order Department
814 North Franklin Street
Chicago, IL 60610
USA
Tel.: +1 800 888 4741 (toll free) | Fax: +1 312 337 5985
Email: orders@ipgbook.com

A Short History of Legal Validity and Invalidity. Foundations of Private and Public Law

ISBN 978-1-78068-815-2
D/2019/7849/88
NUR 820

British Library Cataloguing in Publication Data. A catalogue record for this book is available from the British Library.

For Josep Maria P.

ACKNOWLEDGEMENTS

This short book has a long history, which colleagues in different countries have been part of. Kristin Boosfeld, John Finnis, Birke Häcker, Nils Jansen, Ewan Smith, Paul Yowell and Reinhard Zimmermann at various stages provided very valuable comments on drafts of this book. I benefitted from the feedback of the audiences at the Oxford Comparative Law Discussion Group, the Max-Planck-Institut für ausländisches und internationales Privatrecht, and the Westfälische Wilhelms-Universität Münster, where I was invited to present parts of the manuscript. Brian Lapsa and José Manuel Royo generously helped with the Latin. Ann-Christin Maak-Scherpe, of Intersentia Cambridge, inspired the format and title of this book, and was in every way a receptive and knowledgeable publisher. Writing up the book was made possible by the support of a Research Fellowship at the Programme for the Foundations of Law and Constitutional Government of the Oxford Faculty of Law.

Cover and inside illustrations are by my mother, Trini Tinturé.

MKT
April 2019

CONTENTS

ABBREVIATIONS OF CLASSICAL WORKS

ROMAN LAW

Institutes of Gaius	Gaius, *Institutes*, [book] 2, [section] 146
Rules of Ulpian	Ulpian, *Rules*, [title] 24, [section] 32
Code of Justinian	Justinian, *Code*, [book] 1, [title] 14, [section] 5
Digest of Justinian	Justinian, *Digest*, [book] 40, [title] 9, [section] 16, [paragraph] 1
Institutes of Justinian	Justinian, *Institutes*, [book] 2, [title] 1, [section] 10

MEDIEVAL CANON LAW

Gratian, *Concordia Discordantium Canonum*, Parts I and III	Gratian, *Decretum*, D. [Distinctio] 10, c. [capitulum] 10
Gratian, *Concordia Discordantium Canonum*, Part II	Gratian, *Decretum*, C. [Causa] 7, q. [quaestio] 1, c. [capitulum] 20
Decretals of Pope Gregory IX	Pope Gregory IX, *Decretals*, [book] 1, [title] 3, [chapter] 22

LATER WORKS

Bartolus, *Commentaria in primam Digesti veteris partem, ad Digestum 1, 1, 9*	Bartolus, *Commentary to [Justinian's] Digest, 1, 1, 9*, s. [section] 1
Bartolus, *Commentaria in primam Digesti veteris partem, ad Digestum 1, 3, 23*	Bartolus, *Commentary to [Justinian's] Digest, 1, 3, 23*, s. [section] 31

Bartolus, *Commentaria in primam Codicis partem, ad Codex 1, 1, 1*	Bartolus, *Commentary to [Justinian's] Code, 1, 1, 1,* s. [section] 13
F de Suarez, *Tractatus De Legibus ac Deo Legislatore* (Coimbra: 1612)	Suarez, *De Legibus*, [book] 1, [chapter] 15, [section] 1
FC von Savigny, *System des heutigen Römischen Rechts* (Berlin: 1840–9)	Savigny, *System*, para [paragraph] 23

A STORY IN A (VERY ALLEGORICAL) PICTURE

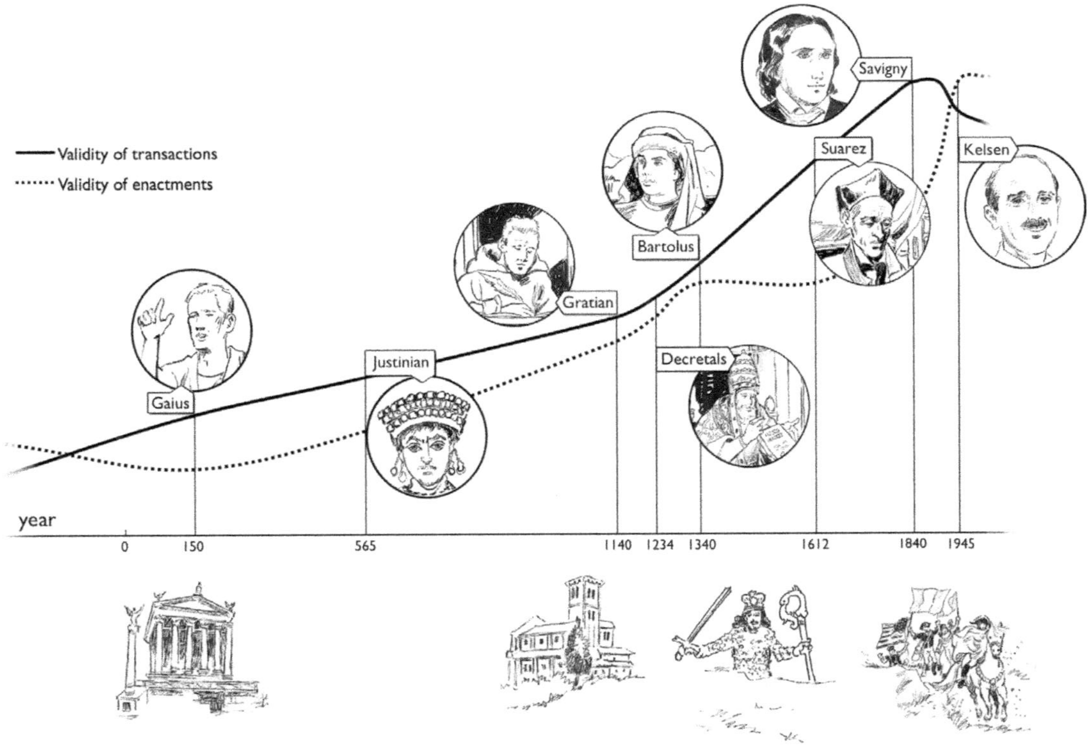

CHAPTER 1
INTRODUCTION

Legal validity and invalidity are central categories of legal thought. Many important matters in legal practice, and therefore in the lives of many persons, turn on whether something is legally valid – for example a mortgage contract, a will, a tax regulation, a judgment, a patent or a planning licence. Scholars and practitioners in any field of law pay considerable attention to what it takes for certain kinds of decision, transaction or enactment to be legally valid, and much argument in court turns on precisely this question. Even our ordinary endeavours are shaped in countless ways by reliance on a myriad of legally valid things, including job appointments, credit cards, bus tickets, passports and PIN codes. The twin ideas of validity and invalidity are so pervasive that in some areas of law specialist vocabulary has developed to discuss problems they give rise to. Thus lawyers may ask, for example, whether a statute is 'constitutional', whether a promise is 'enforceable', or whether a council has acted 'ultra vires', by way of framing enquiries that could principle be translated into more generic 'validity' talk. The language of validity and invalidity is a common denominator that, with differences of emphasis, runs across many varied branches of law, public and private, national and supranational. It is part of the basic grammar shared by traditions of Western legal thought.

Despite its ubiquity in legal scholarship and practice, or perhaps because of it, relatively little attention has been paid to the purpose or rationale of appealing to validity as a warrant for settling pressing social quandaries. Focus on *whether* something is valid, on *criteria* of validity, has largely eclipsed the question *what* validity is and, crucially, *why*, if at all, it can be justified to assign such a decisive place in our dealings to decisions that bear validity's seal. This is a seal that may not attest to justice or moral rightness, but that first and foremost attests to conformity with a set of often arbitrary and formal criteria, criteria set forth in further legal decisions (such as statutes and judgments) which are legally valid themselves.

Nor has legal theory helped to shed light on these neglected questions about legal validity. Mirroring ordinary legal reasoning, legal theorists in recent times have devoted much attention to pondering the nature of validity criteria, abstracting and generalising in various ways from the specifics of lawyerly practice – indeed abstracting from these specifics to the point of taking as the primary object of analysis legal rules or norms, rather than (also) stock transactions, wills or treaty agreements. Thus it is that scholars and students of legal theory today have largely come to associate the idea of legal validity with the Hartian 'rule of recognition'[1] or the Kelsenian 'basic norm',[2] which in different ways embody or represent the *criteria* determining when *rules* or *norms* are legally valid. For all their valuable contributions to legal thought, these lines of literature, and others in their wake, have confined general discussion of validity to an artificially narrow terrain, a terrain at some distance from the realities of lawyerly craft and the intriguing puzzles they throw up – particularly in an age of emerging legal orders, shifting forms of administration, and fresh challenges to the regulation of transactions and exchanges in a digitally scripted world.

The purpose of this book is to help place the neglected questions about legal validity firmly on the scholarly agenda. The book is not itself an exercise in legal theory. Rather it conducts an enquiry that in some ways

1 HLA Hart, *The Concept of Law*, 2nd edn (Oxford, Clarendon Press, 1994) chapter 6.

2 H Kelsen, *General Theory of Law and State*, A Wedberg (tr) (New York, Russell, 1945) 110ff.

is foundational to sound reflection on legal validity in any field of legal research, legal theory included. The book searches for validity's roots, buried deep in European legal culture. It finds and follows the roots of validity as they are nourished and developed in historical scenarios of various kinds, some of which the modern reader might not expect. The book traces a history of legal validity, but it is a history drawn up for a purpose, and which proves revealing to that end. For it reveals *why*, not only when, legal validity emerged as a technique to enable persons and groups to effect social and political transformations that we have grown to take for granted and build upon, but that one day were no less imposing, no less uncharted ground, than many of the developments contemporary legal scholars grapple with. These include European legal integration, which, as we will see, validity has helped to forge for nearly two millennia.

This book will take the reader through a series of strategic developments in Western legal culture, divided up into the book's seven core chapters (chapters 3–9). We will start in Roman law and finish in our days, which are, as one might put it, the immediate aftermath of modern codification and constitutionalism. In between, European legal culture takes many twists and turns. Only some of them are relevant to tracing the origins of validity's craft. And only some of those are made the object of our enquiry. The selected juristic texts are such that, by reason of their nature as positive law or their author's theoretical intentions, they can be expected to engage as profusely with legal validity as befits the legal thought of their time. All studied texts are landmark texts, but not all landmark texts are studied.

The journey will take us not only through different historical periods, but also through different countries and different fields of law. Indeed, one of the most significant findings of this work is that, contrary to what it is often assumed, the idea of legal validity emerged in the domain of private transactions and relationships, and was only gradually extended to the domain of official power and eventually law-making – once, that is, legal thought had embraced the possibility that law-making *itself* could be (in)valid, because *legally limited*, most recently by a body of constitutionally enshrined human rights. This fascinating projection of the logic of validity from the domain of private power to the domain of public power, this transition of validity from being a tool to mould private relations to being a tool to mould law itself, is a progressively incubated turning point of Western legal history that reaches its high-water mark about 200 years ago, hand in hand with the rise of codification and constitutionalism.

And this development, incidentally, helps to explain why, of the nearly two millennia that legal thought has been deploying the grammar of legal validity and invalidity, only the last couple of centuries have figured sustained discussion of the validity of *rules* or *norms*. The latter, understood as the abstracted products of law-making acts, are liable to being (in)valid insofar as the underlying acts are liable to be. Theoretical focus on legally valid norms and their criteria is an offshoot, perhaps a creature, of modern constitutionalism.

Embarking on this journey does not require specialist knowledge of Roman law or legal history. On the contrary, the reader will hopefully find that this guided tour charting the footsteps of legal validity has the welcome side-effect of yielding insights and anecdotes of wider historical interest. The same goes for knowledge of Latin, the language in which most of the studied works were originally drafted. When Latin terms are used in the text, they are always translated. And they are primarily used when the terms themselves tell part of the story. This is true especially of the term-family from which 'validity' directly stems. This linguistic development is instructive and easy to appreciate. Anyone who has been long enough in Spain will have heard locals saying '*vale*' to each other, in expressing agreement or acknowledgment. '*Vale*' is the Spanish 'OK'. Language authorities during the Franco dictatorship, in the twentieth century, endorsed its use with the likely aim of blocking the (Hollywood-driven) spread of 'OK', regarded as an undue foreign influence. Though a relatively new word, the interjection '*vale*' has a long pedigree in Romance languages. It comes straight from the Latin verb '*valere*', which roughly means being physically strong, healthy or fit for purpose.[3] This Latin verb can be used in an extraordinarily broad range of contexts, not unlike '[it is] OK'. '*Valere*', as we will see, is not originally a legal term of art. It becomes one. Or rather, it gives rise to legal terms of art. It is in the Middle Ages that jurists, in search of a uniform label for different kinds of act that are (so to speak) 'legally OK', create the noun '*validitas*' – something like 'OK-ness'. That is the linguistic forefather of 'validity'.

---

3 It has survived in modern European languages in a number of ways that closely track its original meaning (including as the Spanish multi-purpose verb '*valer*'). Hence also the traditional farewell formula '*vale*', built from the imperative 'be well'. This farewell formula is now outdated, although we continue to speak of, for example, *vale*dictory lectures.

But in searching for traces of legal validity in old legal texts we search for more than just a word or family of words. We search for what I have earlier described, loosely, as a technique or tool for changing legal relationships. Although this book's research will ultimately *help* to clarify what validity is, because it will show the consistent role it has played in the reasoning of many generations of jurists, the research must, from the outset, *presuppose* at least a rough notion of what it is that one is looking for when one is looking for legal validity. To that end, chapter 2 briefly sets out an account of the technique of legal validity as we know it today, which underlies the making of anything from valid contracts to valid marriages to valid statutes. The account draws on ideas expounded in greater depth in my work *Legal Validity: The Fabric of Justice*.[4] Very succinctly, the technique of legal validity can be captured by saying that legally valid acts have the (i) *result* of changing legal duties, rights and powers, which result is achieved in a certain (ii) *way*, namely by the agent saying so ('I hereby …'), and subject to certain (iii) *conditions* set by the (iv) legal *system*, wherein the result can (v) *circulate* under the description of a special (vi) *name*, 'legally valid'. Equipped with a basic grasp of what validity is, we will, from chapter 3 onwards, peruse different core texts in search of cues that signal the presence of validity's elements. The *name* 'validity' (vi), as we will see, is perhaps the element that takes longest to stabilise. It does so at the point, in the late Middle Ages, when the underlying technique has grown robust enough that the tip of its iceberg has broken through to the surface of legal terminology. But before and after that some important developments need recounting.

This is, therefore, the route that our journey will follow. Our starting point is Roman law. This is the body of law that built up in the course of a millennium's worth of Roman history, roughly from the fifth century BC to the sixth century AD. Chapters 3 and 4 canvass the idea of legal validity in, respectively, Roman private law and Roman law-making. In the latter domain only the slightest of validity's stirrings will be detected. In fact, in each historical period surveyed in this book, we will appreciate how the development of validity in the public domain lags behind its development in the private domain, until in the modern era the tables

4 M Köpcke, *Legal Validity: The Fabric of Justice* (Oxford, Hart Publishing, 2019) chapter 3.

are turned. In order to mark this evolution, my discussion throughout the book will invoke the inevitably blunt distinction between the field of private law and the field of law-making, with qualifications at relevant points. This broad distinction is found already in the Roman legal universe.

Chapters 5 and 6 take us to the Middle Ages. Here we will explore a pioneering use of legal validity by a group of lawyers engaged in setting up what is at that point a novel kind of political organisation, a predecessor of modern state structures on European ground: the Church. In the eleventh century there is a general upsurge in Roman law scholarship in Europe. The old Roman texts are found (or thought) to be treasure troves of hidden truths and insights worth unearthing. While many scholars study Roman materials as a focally intellectual exercise, scholars of Church law – known as canon lawyers – are perhaps the first to resolutely put the fruits of that intellectual study to the service of a practical, indeed political goal. Cornerstones in this development are, on the one hand, Gratian's *Decretum* (1140), an unofficial but widely influential restatement of Church rules by (it is said) a monk called Gratian; and, on the other hand, the first official Church codification, eventually known as the *Decretals* of Pope Gregory IX (1234). Chapters 5 and 6 consider them in turn.

Chapter 7 deals with an episode of European history that is a crucial hinge between the medieval order, marked by the fading claims to world rulership of the Holy Roman Empire, and the modern scenario of separate political communities growing increasingly robust. As the Middle Ages draw to a close, a perplexing variety of different legal sources lay claim to governing one and the same population. The sources include, on the one hand, local laws such as the ordinances of city-states, and, on the other, what comes to be called the *ius commune* – literally the European 'common law'.[5] The *ius commune* is a blend of positive law and doctrine, both civil and canon, that grows out of the medieval scholarly engagement with Roman legal materials, which are regarded as an emanation of imperial rule. In the fourteenth century, leading scholar Bartolus of Sassoferrato develops a set of doctrines to determine the relative applicability, even validity, of different legal sources bearing on a particular case. In so doing, he not only carves out principles that will one day mature into private international law.

---

5 On the idea of the *ius commune*, see eg N Jansen, '*Ius commune* (Gemeines Recht)' in J Basedow, KJ Hopt and R Zimmermann (eds), *Handwörterbuch des Europäischen Privatrechts* (Tübingen, Mohr Siebeck, 2009).

He also prepares Western legal thought for its cardinal transition from contemplating a single empire to embracing the dawn of sovereign *jurisdictions*.

In chapter 8 we travel to an environment of consolidating nation states which, however, do not yet have thoroughly systematic legal systems in place. Legal practice and scholarship throughout Europe remain profoundly shaped by the *ius commune*, which is increasingly refined and in various ways infiltrates, supplements or even supersedes local regulations.[6] In the seventeenth century, Spanish scholar Francisco de Suarez writes a treatise, titled *De Legibus* (On Laws) (1612), wherein he ponders the relation between positive law (complete with the *ius commune*) and the requirements of right reason ('natural law'). He provides a ground-breaking account of the nature and purpose of the positive laws that regulate the making of valid transactions, which acts he regards as exercises of a power inherent in human beings.

Friedrich Carl von Savigny's reworking of private law (1840–9) introduces the last segment of our historical itinerary, chapter 9, corresponding to the period of modern codification and constitutionalism. Here old crafts acquire new meanings. Despite Savigny's scornful take-down of legislative law-making, or perhaps building on it, the grammar of validity is eventually capitalised on by lawyers in the emerging discipline of public (and administrative) law, and more generally by scholars pursuing and elaborating the ideal of the *Rechtsstaat* or law-governed state – a state, in other words, both legally self-regulating and self-limiting, wherein it is apt to regard *law-making itself as a creature of law*.

This basic logic of constitutionalism, so deeply ingrained in our legal imagination, is in an important sense just another application of a longstanding legal technique in response to social needs which in one sense are novel, but in another sense bear a striking resemblance to the needs that validity has addressed at different stages of its evolution, and remains fit to serve today. These needs and uses of validity are canvassed in the book's concluding chapter 10. The overarching plot of the story

6 On the manifold kinds of 'Reception' process of Roman law, see eg T Duve, 'Von der Europäischen Rechtsgeschichte zu einer Rechtsgeschichte Europas in globalhistorischer Perspektive' (2012) 20 *Rechtsgeschichte* 18, especially 31ff; MT Fögen and G Teubner, 'Rechtstransfer' (2005) 7 *Rechtsgeschichte* 38.

portrayed in the book involves entrusting persons with an ability to make and unmake legal relations by means of their intentional, targeted say-so. It involves, therefore, empowering persons to bind themselves to others, to forge partnerships and assume responsibilities, and otherwise to cast just dealings in legal clothing by way of shaping their own life path and identity as individuals and groups. In the final analysis, this is why Roman jurists devise incipient strategies for individuals to enter and change private arrangements, circumventing the restrictions imposed by archaic Roman rules. This is why medieval canon lawyers rework Church law to make room for new legal developments at the hands of different persons and institutions within the Church hierarchy, and why Bartolus reworks secular law to make room for sovereign legislation by nascent city-states. It is a concern with individual autonomy, in turn, that goes to motivate Suarez's and Savigny's elaborate conception of the strategies and limits of the exercise of private power. And the age of constitutionalism resorts to validity to meet the need – especially post-WWII – for legally binding constraints on the prized expression of democratic will.

It is not by chance that during the greatest part of this long evolution, the use of validity is predominantly confined to the private law domain. The fact that Roman political power is more often usurped than conferred, the assumed divine origin of law in the eyes of canon and Natural Law jurists, the long-unquestioned validity of the *ius commune*, and the Historical School's belief that law is diffusely bred in a 'people's spirit', all contribute to delaying the moment in which legal thought generalises its view of law as itself made through an intentional say-so, as itself a valid artefact of legal technique, akin in this sense to private transactions. Indeed, for not unrelated reasons, for centuries legal thought operates on the assumption that the very power to make transactions is somehow pre-legal rather than legal, somehow natural rather than artificial, so that the role of legal rules is to *remove* or *restrain* an ability that exists independently of them. (Thus, a law requiring a will to have X witnesses presupposes a kind of natural power of testation.) Consistently with this, the historically pioneering discussions of validity in private law are focused, negatively, on the *in*validity of transactions. In a sense to be explained, the history of legal validity is the tale of a transition from power curbed to power conferred.

None of this is to suggest that the technique of validity is unqualifiedly superior to other ways of making law or otherwise altering legal relations.

On the contrary, part of the value of the present study lies in demonstrating how the technique of validity long existed side by side with modes of legal change based on custom formation or the widespread acknowledgement of the authority of texts originally devised as statements of existing law rather than sources of new one. Contemporary scholars seeking to articulate a new European *ius commune* on the back of a shared Roman heritage, or to project the logic of constitutionalism to international treaties, human rights covenants or non-state practices or regulations of various sorts, grapple with predicaments not altogether different from the predicaments once faced by Roman, medieval and early modern jurists.

It is from this struggle to weave harmony within diversity that European legal culture emerged. It is this history that reveals the foundations of validity's craft.

CHAPTER 2
OUR TECHNIQUE OF LEGAL VALIDITY

I. BEYOND 'VALIDITY' TALK

It might seem a strange suggestion that we should think of legal validity as a *technique*. Is legal validity not a *concept*, a fundamental *category* of legal thought? We have been taught that legal validity is a quality of norms or rules. Legally valid norms are part of a legal system. Legal validity is that of which Hart's 'rule of recognition', or Kelsen's 'basic norm', is said to provide the supreme test, in setting criteria for the validity of further norms.[1] Philosophical literature has extensively pondered the necessary

1 HLA Hart, *The Concept of Law*, 2nd edn (Oxford, Clarendon Press, 1994) 105ff; H Kelsen, *General Theory of Law and State*, A Wedberg (tr) (New York, Russell, 1945) 110ff, 115ff, 395–6.

or possible content of criteria of validity of a system's legal norms. Legal validity seems a fertile topic for abstract reflection. But a technique?

A more lawyerly perspective yields a richer picture. In our daily endeavours we come across a myriad of legally valid objects: valid contracts, valid job appointments, valid planning licences, valid judgments, valid pension grants. Lawyers can offer specialist advice on how to validly *make* or *issue* them. Plainly these things are artefacts. They are products of human craft. So, too, are the norms that theorists speak of as 'legally valid'. As Hart, Kelsen and consonant voices will insist, legally valid norms are more or less direct results of an enacting ('positing') choice. Lawyers are used to checking whether purported contracts, resolutions or enactments are valid. The validity of these things turns to a significant extent, and sometimes almost exclusively, on the process whereby they have come into being. The result is valid if the process has been valid itself. Has there been a valid vote, a timely hearing, proper attestation? Validity is somehow associated with the performance of certain procedural steps, of certain *acts*, that in turn have legal consequences.

But not all kinds of act that have legal consequences are naturally spoken of as 'legally valid' – or 'invalid' for that matter. If I commit a crime, a host of new duties, rights and powers become incumbent upon me, not least in relation to the detention, trial and punishment I become liable to undergo, as administered by officials and others whose legal duties, rights and powers accordingly change in complex ways. Entering a contract, too, changes my own and other people's legal rights, duties and powers. That much is common to crimes and valid dealings: they introduce changes in the normative landscape according to law. They yield what I will call *changes in normative positions* (or changes in legal positions). It might be thought that the relevant difference lies in the fact that crimes, unlike contracts, are prohibited by law. That the relevant conduct is unlawful. But that is beside the point. For one thing, it is possible for contracts and other transactions to be prohibited by law and *nevertheless* be legally valid. A thief may under certain circumstances validly transfer title, even though it is a crime to handle stolen goods. For another thing, there are numerous instances of lawful conduct that changes legal positions despite not being aptly described in the language of validity. The act of moving home, by transporting one's belongings from one of one's houses to another, is not as such valid or invalid. Yet it may alter one's entitlements and liabilities in matters of municipal services or local tax.

If we wish to understand what is distinctive of the kinds of act and artefact we standardly refer to as 'valid' or 'invalid', we must look beyond the normative result that these acts yield, and beyond any prohibition or permission attaching to them. We must also look beyond the characteristics of the agent: as with other kinds of act, there are valid acts which are private, such as marriages, and valid acts which are official, such as judgments; there are valid acts made individually, such as wills, and valid acts made collectively, such as company mergers. If we are to explain why, as my remarks have been assuming, our entrenched talk of 'validity' and 'invalidity' across different fields of law is more than just a haphazard or random linguistic habit, we must be able to point to some legally relevant feature or set of features peculiar to things we regularly so call, and only to them. We must be able to show that there is something distinctive, as a matter of law, about the things we habitually call legally 'valid' and 'invalid' – something other than the fact that we so call them.

I have elsewhere raised and defended the hypothesis that there *is* something distinctive and important about valid doings.[2] The distinctive mark of valid doings is not that they change legal positions, or which legal positions they change. The distinctive mark of valid doings is *how* they change legal positions. The hypothesis, in other words, is that there is something peculiar to the *way* in which certain acts change legal positions, and that these are the acts we habitually speak of as being 'valid' or as giving rise to 'valid' objects. Thus regarded, the language of 'validity' is a surface mark of an underlying kinship. It is that kinship that both lawyers and theorists would do well to attend to. Because it has to do with the manner in which one goes about producing normative results, I call this kinship a legal *technique*.

The thesis of this book is that the technique of legal validity develops hand in hand with Western legal culture. It emerges over 2,000 years of European history and helps to steer that history's course. The present chapter lays the foundations for this historical investigation by articulating the main features of the technique of validity, as we know it today. For, inevitably, the historical journey must presuppose a preliminary understanding of

---

2 M Köpcke, *Legal Validity: The Fabric of Justice* (Oxford, Hart Publishing, 2019), especially chapters 2, 3 and 6.

what it is that we look for when we look for the origins *of legal validity*. This preliminary understanding will enable us to trace the evolution of the technique of validity across different phases of our legal culture – for example, by detecting early or incipient forms of the technique, or by appreciating why some of its features are only eventually added or consolidated. The historical study, in turn, will go to confirm the existence and nature of the technique. It will demonstrate how the various features of this technique, pointed up in the next section, have tended to operate in combination, even across profoundly different social and political environments – different amongst themselves, and different from our own.

It is not insignificant that valid doings broadly correspond to what a recent body of literature calls 'exercises of legal power', governed by 'power-conferring rules'.[3] Despite using such terminology, this body of literature has consistently failed to bring out in what sense legal power is *power*, and how it is that legal rules *confer* it. The answer, as we will see, lies in the workings of the technique, which are magnificently illustrated by its history. There is a reason why validity was appealed to and relied on at defining junctures of our legal lineage. The technique of validity places in the hands of those who use it an extraordinary capacity, a capacity to shape legal relations through a deliberate, targeted and relatively simple act. Understanding the nature of the technique, this book shows, is closely bound up with understanding how it is a tool for allocating power – for both bestowing and limiting it.

II. SIX MAIN FEATURES

The main features of the technique of legal validity can be grouped into six broad kinds, which build on one another. They may be jointly captured by saying that a legally valid act

(i) has the *result* of changing normative positions (legal rights, duties, powers), which result is brought about
(ii) in a certain *way*, namely (roughly) by the agent saying so, and

---

3 The most prominent source of the received idea of legal power is probably Hart's work (Hart, *The Concept of Law*, 27ff). For a critical overview of the received idea, see Köpcke, *Legal Validity*, chapter 2.

(iii) subject to certain *conditions or limits* ('criteria')
(iv) set by the law's *systemic* framework, in contemplation of which the result
(v) can *circulate* as a relatively free-standing entity
(vi) under the description of a special *name* ('valid').

Consider each of these features in turn.

(i) The *result* of valid acting is a change in the legal rights, duties and powers of a number of persons, often including persons who were not involved in the performance of the act and might not have witnessed it. This result, as noted already, is common to legally valid conduct and to conduct legally regulated in other ways, for example in being prohibited or permitted. In all these cases, the normative changes produced may be more or less lasting, more or less grievous for some or many, more or less subject to reversal, and due to the acts of either officials or private individuals.

(ii) But legally valid acts change normative positions in a certain *way*. This is their central distinctive mark, to the point that it warrants speaking of a *technique* of validity. All kinds of valid acting, whether public enactments or private contracts, whether ephemeral transactions or momentous treaty agreements, share a basic modus operandi. Roughly put, the agent changes legal positions *by saying so*. More precisely, he changes legal positions by manifesting an intent to change legal positions *through that very manifestation of intent*. This self-referring or reflexive nature of the agent's intent is captured by the lawyerly phrase 'hereby'. To say that 'I *hereby* marry' is to say that I marry *by* doing the very thing I am doing *here* and now – namely, saying that I marry. But also less formal and explicit formulations manifest one's intent to do something by so saying. Operative verbs in legal documents ('appeal *dismissed*', 'Mrs Smith *accepts* the inheritance') describe a normative change in the process of making it. Even non-verbal conduct, including silence, may unequivocally manifest an intention to thereby enter legal relations, in the appropriate context – not unlike ordinary communication can and does fare without words. Placing a bunch of carrots on the shop counter unequivocally, though inexplicitly, conveys 'I wish to buy them'.

This basic modus operandi, described in some private law regimes as a 'declaration of will', is simple yet powerful. It is simple because it essentially involves a self-fulfilling wish. One makes something true by expressing one's wish to make it true. One brings about normative changes – changes in the rights, duties and powers people hold *in law* – by speaking one's own mind. In a sense one has targeted control of the entire legal machinery at one's lips. Therefore the strategy is powerful. What one decides in the present may have an enduring force in the future. What one chooses by oneself may have standing implications for others.

Indeed, in performing a legally valid act, one may rally the *decisions* of others and bring them to bear on one's own. The brief agreement concerning purchase produces a range of intricate normative changes over and above what is ostensibly in the mind of the parties. These include contractual terms that consumer legislation 'implies' into the transaction. Similarly, a resolution awarding citizenship goes nowhere near articulating the colossal normative feat it pulls off, in terms of the normative positions it alters, which the issuing official need not extensively know. Statutes, too, may invoke legal concepts and regimes substantially spelled out in other statutes or in the common law. These and many other forms of valid acting routinely invoke a legal regime crafted earlier and by others. The reason for this is the *systemic* relationship among valid acts in a legal order (feature (iv) below). It entails the familiar need to read together different legal materials in figuring out 'what the law is on' a question.

In many ways this systemic bearing of valid acts on one another goes to buttress the power one wields in using the technique of validity. One can conclude normatively complex operations by manifesting one's wish to carry them out under a very general description only, such as 'marrying Jane' or 'bequeathing my estate to Tom'. One can successfully operate in countless branches of law without specialist knowledge. But there is a flipside. It is that one may sign up to arrangements one would not have wished to endorse. Not everyone reads the terms of financial instruments. And perhaps only conscientious MPs study the bills they vote on. The technique in one's hands is so powerful that it may take over.

It takes over in most dramatic form when one performs a valid act altogether by accident. Pick the wrong ballot paper and you may have supported a motion you meant to oppose. One mouse-click too many, and you may be bound by a transaction you had never meant to enter. There is a standing possibility that legally valid acts are performed wholly or partly unintentionally, a possibility that even doctrines on mistake and procedural safeguards such as warnings and attestation on the whole leave room for. Ironically, this possibility, too, is very much an upshot of the basic *way* in which valid acts are performed. One may perform valid acts unintentionally because acting validly involves *manifesting* an intention. And it does not take an intention to manifest an intention. Given one's outward actions, others may be entitled to rely, in law, on what reasonably looked like a deliberate and informed act, even though it was not.

It follows that changing legal positions by saying so is a powerful technique, which has hazards and costs. It also has limits – but these are picked up by the next feature.

(iii) Most of us cannot give legal clothing to anything we wish, whenever we wish. There are stringent limits both on the kinds of thing we can accomplish through a legally valid act, and on the kinds of procedure whereby we can do so. If you try to make a contract that fundamentally conflicts with public policy, you fail. You likewise fail if you try to convey land on tissue paper, try to make a ruling that is deeply ultra vires, or try to marry a person who is already married. Note that this is the converse scenario from the one just discussed, in which you unintentionally perform a valid act. In the present scenario your intention to change legal positions may be robust and settled. You fail in your attempt to perform a valid act, *notwithstanding* your manifest intention to perform it. The law places conditions on the substance and procedure of your valid action. Legal theorists refer to these conditions as 'criteria of legal validity'.[4]

At first glance, the existence of these conditions appears inherently to *restrict* or *curb* the power one can exercise through a valid act. Arduous and expensive formal requirements and narrowly defined spheres of competence may well be a disruption from the agent's point of view. There can be good reasons, of course, for placing such constraints. Only qualified administrative bodies should take decisions in which technical expertise is key. Parents ought not to be able to validly form marriages for children against their consent. Parliament, not the executive, should change income

---

4 The existence of criteria of validity is compatible with my formulation of the *way* we change legal positions under heading (ii) above. In order to explicitly account for validity criteria, we could say that, in using the technique of validity, we change legal positions *if and to the extent legally provided*, by *legally* manifesting an intention thereby to do so (see Köpcke, *Legal Validity*, 57–9).

tax rates. Judges, not police officers, should issue sentences. Criteria of validity are privileged tools for the allocation of power within a legal system. In the process they can also serve to rein in the performance of wrongful conduct. An act's prohibition, including its criminal prohibition, can be a ground of invalidity. In all the preceding respects, properly deployed criteria of validity look like constraints indeed, albeit justified ones.

But one must not neglect another aspect of this same reality. There is an important sense in which criteria of validity can themselves be empowering, power-*conferring* – echoing the label used in modern jurisprudential literature. The presence of criteria of validity enables us to accomplish things that would otherwise hardly be within our reach. It is thanks to the fact that a conveyance must be executed in a deed and perhaps inscribed in an official registry that it can bear standing witness to the underlying transaction many years after its performance, and vis-à-vis persons who were not part of it, and their heirs, and future judges. Without those procedural requirements, one could not wield a power, now, that generations will be bound to heed. Labour law, on its part, precludes me from validly signing up to exploitative work conditions, and consumer law precludes me from validly agreeing to abusive terms of sale. Here as well, law constrains my freedom to decide, but in so doing it enables me to decide freely. More generally, the law of contract enables me to autonomously forge relationships with others in holding me to my expressed commitments, even those commitments I have come to regret. Sound criteria of validity, in other words, do not so much limit as *delimit*, that is, clarify the boundaries of, reasonable exercises human autonomy.[5]

(iv) The existence of criteria of validity presupposes something more fundamental. It presupposes a legal framework that sets them. Legal validity is *intrasystemic*: it is *relative* to some framework or order. There cannot be a legally valid act in the absence of a governing legal framework, which framework assigns the relevant say-so a legal meaning precisely in determining what it can legally accomplish and how. Such legal framework makes it the case, for example, that certain people gathered in a certain place at a certain time can through their say-so make a legislative enactment

[5] On how criteria of validity can be key to fostering the reasonable self-direction of individuals and groups, see Köpcke, *Legal Validity*, chapters 4–7, especially chapter 5, section VII, and chapter 7, section I.

or enter a marriage, as opposed to merely going through motions devoid of legal import.

But the governing legal framework is, itself, the more or less immediate result of *further* valid acts, typically of others. No doubt, as one follows through the lineage of any binding legal regime there will come a stage at which it no longer makes sense to ask about, or even speak of, the 'validity' of certain foundational arrangements, such as written constitutions or constitutional conventions – unless, that is, one is prepared to postulate a hypothetical master-norm in the way that Kelsen proposed. In propounding his 'basic norm', Kelsen formalised an assumption that is deeply entrenched in everyday legal reasoning. For, in speaking of something as 'valid', one implicitly presupposes the existence of a *validating* framework or rule.

The fact that criteria of validity are ultimately determined by other human acts entails, in turn, that such criteria will not necessarily track principles of justice or succeed in precluding that unjust dealings are validly made. There can therefore be no truth in any general denial of the possibility of unjust legally valid laws, or for that matter of unjust legally valid wills, marriages or judgments. Legal thinkers who have sought to mask this reality, such as Suarez (chapter 8.III–IV), have got trapped in argumentative confusions, if not contradictions. Indeed, as we will see, law's ability to regulate the conditions under which valid law itself is made had long been played down in Western legal culture, until in the last two centuries this reality became central to scholarly thought (chapter 9.II–III). That there is law about law, that law regulates its own creation, that law an object of legal making – these are now familiar ideas, popularised by jurisprudential writers, and silently running through entire branches of law, constitutional and administrative law in particular. The praise of the Rule of Law or the law-governed state (*Rechtsstaat*) is, in a sense, an exaltation of a feature of legal validity that has been present, to some degree, since the technique's inception in private law.

(v) Valid choosing acts are one-off events, which lie in the past as soon as they are performed. But the subsisting legal system assigns to them continuing legal relevance. An old conveyance remains a source of legal rights, powers and duties not only because it was originally executed in proper form, but also because today's law continues to recognise as valid now what was validly made then. Given the enduring legal relevance of valid choices, the need arises for effective ways to identify them through time, relatively independently of the circumstances of their making and even of the identity of their makers. The need arises for valid choices to *circulate*.

Criteria of validity may themselves facilitate the circulation of valid choices. Legal determination of procedure and form can secure reliance, thanks to special identifying marks in some cases associated to documentary supports such as deeds, registries or governmental gazettes, or to physical tokens such as passports, credit cards, bus tickets or licence plates. Such physical tokens are curious objects indeed. We speak of them, too, as 'legally valid'. They even seem to have their own criteria of validity, which need not coincide with those of the underlying transaction or resolution. These objects are proofs of an underlying act. They are something like portable normative changes. You carry them in your pocket. They capture the most literal sense in which valid choices may be said to circulate.

But such physical circulation only buttresses the *legal* circulation that valid choices are capable of. This legal circulation has a familiar linguistic counterpart. There is a dedicated conceptual apparatus to refer to the sets of normative changes that valid acts give rise to – to refer to them, that is, in relative isolation of their originating context, almost as subsisting entities. We often speak of a 'contract', an 'enactment' or a 'licence' not in reference to a past, datable act, but as shorthand for a bundle of legal positions that bears on our legal status in the present ('the contract entitles me to …'). It is no coincidence that this form of vocabulary involves nominalised verbs (to contract/contract, to enact/enactment, to license/licence, to marry/marriage, to judge/judgment, to appoint/appointment, to resolve/resolution, etc). As I suggested at the start of this chapter, there is a *process-product ambiguity* inherent in valid acting. Legal validity, in other words, colours not only a result but also the process whereby it is arrived at. The same is plainly not true of many other properties of things. One can quickly build a fast car, but the speed of the process need have no bearing on the speed of the product. In law, however, the validity of the process spills over to, and determines, the validity of the product. For the valid product is, in a sense, just an embodiment of the valid act. 'Contract', 'enactment' and 'licence' designate normative changes that result from the acts of contract*ing*, enact*ing* and licens*ing*. These are normative changes marked by reason of their source.

Ultimately, the legal circulation of these sources of rights and duties is made possible by a set of legal doctrines that jointly assign lasting significance to the original choice. They include tightly circumscribed regimes of frustration and rescission, limited stages of appeal and grounds thereof, and other barriers to the retroactive scope of normative changes, with doctrines of finality and presumptions of validity operating in the background. In fact, where certainty is key, compliance with certain sophisticated procedural steps may conclusively override, as a matter of law, any substantive flaws in the underlying arrangement. This is so, for example, with certain forms of registry entry or deed. Here formal criteria of validity go to *guarantee* a normative change, hand in hand with facilitating its identification.

(vi) The five preceding features make up a legal technique, a way of crafting normative changes, of which the language of 'validity' and 'invalidity' is a symptom. But it is more than just a symptom. The binary, uniform terminology of 'validity' and 'invalidity' (complete with its cognate expressions) itself aids the identification of valid results. It helps the demarcation of rights, duties and powers by reason of their *source*. For this is not the only kind of demarcation that we use in legal argument. We often bundle normative positions by reason of the *situation* on which they bear. We may accordingly speak of, say, 'the GBH rule' or 'the mailbox rule' to refer to a legal regime that has come together through a combination of legislative, judicial and other valid decisions at various points in time. Although we sometimes give norms or rules the name of a case in which they were prominently developed, as in 'the rule of *Rylands v Fletcher*', the cumulative mechanics of *stare decisis*, notably in some jurisdictions, rarely makes it the case that any such 'rule' results exclusively from a discrete judicial decision, especially when the line of precedents is tortuous and long. Speaking of 'the rule in *Rylands v Fletcher*' as a 'legally valid norm' may accordingly seem to some, and rightly so, a stretch of language. The language of validity is more naturally associated to *acts* than to rules, except where the latter bear close to a one-to-one relationship to an originating say-so.

This is ultimately why legal theorists' focus on the validity of rules or norms obscures not only the rich systemic relations between valid acts, but also the remarkable technique whereby they are performed in all areas of legal regulation – not only, or even paradigmatically, by a single law-maker able to 'posit' norms on a clean slate.

This section's outline of the technique of validity helps us understand the legal distinctness of valid acts vis-à-vis other kinds of conduct that alter legal positions. One does not move home by so saying, any more than one commits a wrong simply by expressing one's wish to incur liability (feature (ii)). And while there will be conditions circumscribing any form of conduct that has legal consequences (feature (iii)), as per the system's relevant (criminal, tax, etc) regime on point (feature (iv)), the normative changes which result from the conduct's performance do not have the capacity to circulate that is inherent in valid objects (feature (v)). Of course the fact that one committed a crime in the past may have legal significance in the future, but we do not think of a committed crime as a subsisting entity, apt to be referred to and circulate in isolation of the person committing it, as if it could be carried in one's briefcase. It is the combined interplay of these features that yields a distinct legal technique.

Of this legal technique we now search the roots. Tracing them will shed new light on how its features hang together and, more intriguingly, on the sense in which valid action, both official and private, can amount to an exercise of *power*.

CHAPTER 3
ROMAN PRIVATE LAW
Rowing Against the Tide

We begin our search for validity's roots in the Roman civilisation. 'Roman law' refers to the legal provisions and practices that developed from the early Roman Republic, in the fifth century BC, to Justinian's compilation, in the sixth century AD. Although this is a time span of about 1,000 years, during which one might expect substantial changes in the rules and practices to occur, the chief surviving evidence of the law of this long period is precisely the compilation commissioned by Emperor Justinian, the very text that, in a sense, brings the period to an end.[1] The compilation is made up of several works, known as the Digest, Institutes, Code and Novels (later jointly called *Corpus Iuris Civilis*). The first two in particular purport to recover the best of classical Roman law, as expressed in the writings of Roman jurists such as Gaius, Ulpian or Modestinus in the second and

[1] On Justinian's compilation, see chapter 5.I below.

third centuries AD. But the compilation in many cases collates and condenses materials in unsystematic ways, and only some pieces of juristic writing have reached us in their original form. As a result, identifying the precise content and timing of a Roman rule often enough gives rise to a riddle.

It may have done so even in Roman times. For a remarkable feature of the Roman legal order, especially in its classical period,[2] is that it lacks anything close to an arrangement of law-making sources of the kind we would find in a contemporary state. Legislative power fluctuates between various institutions, while, at the same time, the old body of civil law (*ius civile*), itself a blend of custom and enactments, becomes gradually supplemented by a more modern body of law arising from the piecemeal activity of magistrates, known as praetors, who are in charge of the administration of justice (*ius honorarium*).[3]

But just this complex structural makeup of the Roman legal order, as we will see, creates the need for a technique to make and unmake legal relationships in a relatively reliable and targeted fashion. What in one sense are obstacles to the use of such technique become the reason and chief motivation for its development. This is particularly so in the domain of private law, the object of this chapter.

I. ULPIAN'S ENIGMATIC CLASSIFICATION

Textbooks on Roman law often speak of the validity or invalidity of private transactions such as contracts or wills. While it is well understood that the abstract idea of a *transaction* is absent from Roman legal thought,[4] textbook discussions frequently convey the impression that Romans do operate with a robust idea of *validity* (and *invalidity*). It should surprise us to learn that Romans use a technical notion of legal validity. The practically minded Roman jurist is not prone to devising abstract concepts, concerned as he

2 The rules that classical Roman jurists systematise and bear witness to in the second and third centuries AD (during the Principate) were incubated during the last two centuries BC (in the late Republic). In a broad sense, therefore, Roman law's 'classical period' covers this entire time span.

3 On the *ius honorarium* (praetorian law), see chapter 4.III below.

4 On Savigny's development of the idea of a transaction (*Rechtsgeschäft*), see chapter 9.I below.

is to establish whether or not a claim (*actio*) is available under certain circumstances. Still, the view that Romans have a stable category of legal validity is not groundless. A cursory look at classical materials appears to vindicate it. At the very start of a treatise by Ulpian we find what looks like an account of legislative invalidation of transactions. Ulpian explains how different kinds of Roman statutes (*leges*) bear on (what we must understand to be) private transactions of unnamed kinds. This intriguing passage, as reconstructed, reads as follows:

> A *lex* is either *perfecta*, or *imperfecta*, or *minus quam perfecta*. A *lex perfecta* is one which forbids [*vetat*] something to be done, and rescinds [*rescindit*] it if it be done … A *lex imperfecta* is one which forbids something to be done, and yet, if it be done, neither rescinds it nor imposes a penalty on him who has acted contrary to the law … A *lex minus quam perfecta* is one which forbids something to be done, and if it be done does not rescind it, but imposes a penalty on him who has acted contrary to the law …[5]

So Ulpian distinguishes three types of *leges* in terms of how they legally bear on transactions they concern. All three types of *leges* prohibit certain kinds of transactions. *Leges perfectae* ('perfect laws'), he says, both prohibit and 'rescind' the relevant transaction. *Leges minus quam perfectae* ('laws that are short of perfect') do not 'rescind' but only penalise prohibited transactions. *Leges imperfectae* ('imperfect laws') simply prohibit.

It is tempting to read Ulpian as invoking the contemporary contrast between prohibition and invalidity, canvassed in chapter 2 above. Hart famously stressed, and we generally accept today, that a certain act may be both prohibited and valid, or indeed both prohibited and *in*valid.[6] We understand that the two categories, validity and prohibition, cut across one another, and this is, inter alia, because we have a well-settled idea of legal validity which our idea of prohibition is contrasted *to*.

---

5 *Rules of Ulpian* (Ulpian, *Rules*), [title] 1, [sections] 1–2 (*Lex aut perfecta est, aut imperfecta, aut minus quam perfecta. Perfecta lex est, quae vetat aliquid fieri, et si factum sit, rescindit … Imperfecta lex est, quae vetat aliquid fieri, et si factum sit, nec rescindit, nec poenam iniungit ei, qui contra legem fecit … Minus quam perfecta lex est, quae vetat aliquid fieri, et si factum sit, non rescindit, sed poenam iniungit ei, qui contra legem fecit …*). My translation is adapted from JT Abdy and B Walker, *The Commentaries of Gaius and the Rules of Ulpian*, 3rd edn (Cambridge, Cambridge University Press, 1885).

6 HLA Hart, *The Concept of Law*, 2nd edn (Oxford, Oxford University Press, 1994) chapter 3, especially 33–5; HLA Hart, *Essays on Bentham: Jurisprudence and Political Theory* (Oxford, Clarendon Press, 1982) 212ff.

But in all likelihood there is no similarly well-settled category of legal validity in Roman private law.[7] A simple linguistic observation might be enough to bring home this point. Roman writings use an extravagantly miscellaneous range of expressions to name, *rather unstably*, the status of various kinds of transactions that fail to yield all or some of their characteristic legal effects. Gaius' discussion of wills provides an illustration.[8] It surveys different kinds of flaws to wills, and eventually pauses, briefly, to reflect on the name to be given to the status of the wills thus flawed. The terms '*irritum*' (of no effect) and '*ruptum*' (broken), Gaius observes, could be used interchangeably in this context, but it is more accurate, he adds, to say of some wills that they were not made according to law (*non iure fieri*), of others that they have been revoked or broken, and so are '*rupta*', and of yet others that they have become '*irrita*' as a result of the maker undergoing a loss of status (*capitis diminutio*).[9] Unfortunately this threefold classification does not match the jargon that Gaius himself has been deploying and will continue to deploy in his treatment of wills. Immediately before this brief terminological reflection, he has said that wills whose maker undergoes *capitis diminutio* are thereby '*infirmantur*' (deprived of strength),[10] the same term he has earlier predicated of a will that omits reference to (ie pretermits) a subsequently born child,[11] although in connection with cases of pretermitted heirs he most often uses the term '*ruptum*' and the verb '*rumpere*' (to break), the latter synonymously with '*rescindere*' (to rescind, break down).[12] Moreover, the terms '*inutile*' (useless) and '*(non) valet*' ((is not) strong, fit for purpose), which he recurrently uses as well throughout the whole discussion, do not appear in his classification at all. Importantly, one cannot discern any stable distinction between the *ideas* invoked through this promiscuous vocabulary. At one point Gaius treats the

---

7 For an argument on point, see eg S Di Paola, *Contributi ad una Teoria della Invalidità e della Inefficacia in Diritto Romano* (Varese, Multa Paucis, 1966), defending that the variegated vocabulary in the Roman sources marks distinctions within the domain of '(in)efficacy' rather than the domain of (in)validity; M Kaser, *Das Römische Privatrecht I: Das Altrömische, das Vorklassische und Klassische Recht* (Munich, C.H. Beck'sche Verlagsbuchhandlung, 1955) 214–9 ('[h]ardly any field of private law is as poorly elaborated by the classics as the ineffectiveness [*Unwirksamkeit*] of transactions', 214); R Zimmermann, *The Law of Obligations: Roman Foundations of the Civilian Tradition* (Cape Town, Juta & Co Ltd, 1990) 678–81.

8 *Institutes of Gaius* (Gaius, *Institutes*), [book] 2, [sections] 101ff. On the unstable classical terminology on flaws to wills, see M Kaser, *Das Römische Privatrecht I*, 577–8.

9 Gaius, *Institutes*, 2, 146.

10 ibid 2, 145.

11 ibid 2, 131.

12 ibid 2, 143.

status of a revoked (*ruptum*) will as being equivalent to the status of a will that simply fails to take effect because (for example) the person instituted declines to be heir: in both cases the will 'has no force' (*nullas vires habet*).[13] And we eventually learn that even wills that are '*irrita*' or '*rupta*' may not be altogether '*inutilia*' thanks to the availability of praetorian remedies.[14]

It is telling that a substantial proportion of this vocabulary bears a close link to the ordinary notions of strength, force, firmness or utility; and elsewhere Roman jurists deploy terms such as '*effectum non habet*' (has no effect) and '*inefficax*' (ineffectual) synonymously with '*non valet*', '*nullum*' (of no account) and others.[15] Those are clearly not juridical terms of art. Jurists moreover alternate between the use of these terms and more or less direct descriptions of the relevant legal consequences, whether by referring to the birth and cancellation of obligations ('*nova nascitur obligatio et prima tollitur*', '*posterior obligatio nulla est*'),[16] or even by describing the ensuing states of affairs, such as the fact that slaves manumitted (freed) in excess of the permitted number 'will not be free' (*nulli liberi erunt*).[17] The palpable lack of a uniform terminological pattern to reflect an organised set of ideas, ideas that not even Gaius' generalising moment of discourse appropriately categorises, advises great caution in taking Ulpian's '*rescindere*', the mark of *leges perfectae*, as connoting a contemporary notion of (in)validity.

But caution would be called for in any case because Ulpian's tripartite classification of *leges* cannot, without more, comfortably match our current understandings. It must surprise the modern reader, for instance, that *leges perfectae* do not also penalise the act that they invalidate and, at the other end of spectrum, that *leges imperfectae* simply prohibit and do no more.

As it turns out, the most plausible explanation of the distinction between the three kinds of *leges* adds credence to our above surmises about legal

13 ibid 2, 144.

14 ibid 2, 147.

15 As shown in Di Paola, *Teoria della Invalidità e della Inefficacia*, especially note 35 at 15.

16 Gaius, *Institutes*, 3, 176 ('a new obligation is born and the first is done away with', 'the subsequent obligation is void'; my translation relies on EA Whittuck (ed) and E Poste (tr), *Gai Institutiones or Institutes of Roman Law by Gaius* (Oxford, Clarendon Press, 1904)).

17 Gaius, *Institutes*, 1, 46, as an expression equivalent to '*rescindit*'; about related predicaments Paulus says that the manumitter '*nihil aget*' (*Digest of Justinian* (Justinian, *Digest*), [book] 40, [title] 9, [section] 16, [paragraph] 1) and Modestinus says that '*[n]ulla competit libertas*' (Justinian, *Digest*, 40, 9, 19).

validity in Roman law. Here, as so often in Roman law, categories must be made sense of by working up from the more specific to the more general. Ulpian himself, in the passage I quoted from, names an example for each of the three kinds of *leges* he lists. Based on these and other, sparse references in the Roman legal materials, we know the main outlines of the legal regime contained in a few prominent instances of *leges* of these different kinds.

The distinction has an important chronological dimension that Ulpian's passage does not disclose. *Leges minus quam perfectae* and *imperfectae* are older forms of legislation; *leges perfectae* begin to be enacted in the late Republic, and eventually supersede their older cognates. Very probably, the reason for this temporal shift is that the two older kinds of *leges* embody legislative techniques designed to achieve or approximate the effect that is later achieved by *leges perfectae*, in the face of certain restrictions on the capacity of older statutes directly to impinge on transactions concluded in accordance with the formal rules of *ius civile*.[18] This touches on a major distinct feature of the old *ius civile*, sometimes referred to as its immutability or formalism. Transactions are perfected through the observance of a set procedure, and once they have thus come into legal existence, they are not amenable to being undone or otherwise affected by statutory prohibitions or other obstacles – at civil law anyway. It will be the praetor's task, of course, to offer solutions to this rigidity, and legislators will capitalise on this possibility. As a result, transactions in legal existence *iure civili* (in contemplation of civil law) may in practice be partially or totally depleted

---

18 For helpful developments of this rationale, as broadly presented here, see M Kaser, *Über Verbotsgesetze und Verbotswidrige Geschäfte im Römischen Recht* (Vienna, Verlag der Österreichischen Akademie der Wissenschaften, 1977) 13–68; Zimmermann, *The Law of Obligations*, 697–701; Di Paola, *Teoria della Invalidità e della Inefficacia*, especially chapter 2. A somewhat narrower explanation (echoed eg in WW Buckland, *A Text-Book of Roman Law from Augustus to Justinian* (Cambridge, Cambridge University Press, 1921) note 2 at 7) focuses on the inability of *plebiscites* to alter the civil law before the *lex Hortensia* (286 BC) bestows on them the status of ordinary legislation; for criticism of this and other alternative explanations, see Kaser, *Verbotsgesetze*, 14–8. It is irrelevant for our purposes whether the distinction between the three kinds of *leges* corresponds to a distinction in the respective *sanctiones* (a *sanctio* formally being the last part of a *lex*, following *praescriptio* and *rogatio*). According to some sources, *sanctiones* set out penalties for breach of the relevant *lex* (Justinian, *Digest*, 48, 19, 41; *Institutes of Justinian* (Justinian, *Institutes*), [book] 2, [title] 1, [section] 10 in fine). It is often said that *leges imperfectae* do not have a *sanctio* (eg PGH Willems, *Droit Public Romain ou Les Institutions Politiques de Rome depuis l'Origin de a Ville jusqu'a Justinian*, 5th edn (Louvain, Peeters, 1833) 184; GF Puchta, *Cursus der Institutionen*, vol I (Leipzig, Breitkopf und Härtel, 1841) 284; O Karlowa, *Römische Rechtsgeschichte I* (Leipzig, Veit und Comp, 1885) 427–8).

of legal effects in virtue of the consolidating body of praetorian law, the *ius honorarium*.

The rationale of *leges minus quam perfectae* must be understood in this context. They are the default measure during Republican times, out of the three we are considering. *Leges minus quam perfectae* prohibit and penalise specific transactions the Roman legislator wishes to discourage. Ulpian names the *lex Furia Testamentaria* (date uncertain), which prohibits legacies exceeding 1,000 asses[19] (with some exemptions) and imposes a penalty of four times the excess. The legacy as such stands, is not 'rescinded'. Gaius reports that this law, and a subsequent one (of 169 BC) forbidding individual legacies to exceed the amount left to the heir, did not sufficiently advance the legislator's purpose of protecting the heir's position, as the rules lent themselves to circumvention through a multiplication of the number of legacies.[20] Only the subsequent *lex Falcidia* (of 40 BC), says Gaius, managed to guarantee for the heir a quarter of the estate by prohibiting the bequest of more than three quarters of it. As this is a *lex perfecta*, legacies in excess of this proportion are cut down pro rata.[21]

As Gaius' reflection implies, the provision in the *lex Furia Testamentaria*, the legislator's first shot at fixing the problem, is closer to being a surrogate rescission than to being a genuine prohibition of an act deemed dishonest or wrongful – a genuine prohibition analogous to, say, the contemporary ban on handling stolen goods, which is compatible with the ensuing transaction remaining legally valid for the sake of countervailing policy considerations of a different order, such as the protection of third parties. Rather, the *lex Furia Testamentaria*, a 'law that is short of perfect', appears to penalise *because it cannot rescind*. The person it penalises, importantly, is the legatee. One may easily lose sight of this given Ulpian's initial generic statement, quoted above, that the penalty is incumbent 'on him who has acted contrary to the law'. It is the legatee, ie the beneficiary, who is penalised, and the penalty entails that he has to pay, indeed pay back – to the heir.[22] Depending on the amount of the surplus, he may effectively have

---

19 The *as* is the basic unit of Roman currency.

20 Gaius, *Institutes*, 2, 225–6. The second-named law is the *lex Voconia*; it is not certain whether it, too, is *lex perfecta* (cf Kaser, *Verbotsgesetze*, 50–3, defending that it is).

21 Gaius, *Institutes*, 2, 227 (likewise Ulpian, *Rules*, 24, 32). If the legacy is incapable of division, the legatee must refund proportionately (Justinian, *Digest*, 35, 2, 80, 1).

22 There seems to have been an additional penalty of *manus iniectio*, but with a legal avenue for the defendant to resist arrest (Gaius, *Institutes*, 4, 23–4).

to pay back all or nearly all the money received. Viewed in this light, the difference between a *lex minus quam perfecta* and a *lex perfecta* – between a law that penalises and one that 'rescinds' – comes close to being a difference in degree, rather than in kind.[23] The penalty imposed by the former comes close to being an indirect strategy for attaining what the latter can bring about more directly. This also explains why it is unnecessary for the *lex perfecta* to add a penalty. At stake is, as standardly in *ius civile*, a unilateral transaction: here a legacy. It is burdensome enough for the beneficiary to have the transaction reversed; more so (in principle) than to lose just a multiple of the surplus.

The place of *leges imperfectae* fits the above picture. *Leges imperfectae* are only exceptionally resorted to in Republican times, and eventually not at all. The most cited example of a *lex imperfecta*, and also Ulpian's, is the *lex Cincia* (about 204 BC). The *lex Cincia* prohibits gifts exceeding a certain amount, but attaches no penalty. This is because (part of) the point of this law, upon credible conjecture, is to curb an extended practice whereby members of the leading circles of society will extract, in exchange for their services, not always voluntary 'gifts' from others.[24] One has to bear in mind that, somewhat cynically, in Rome it is deemed improper for 'liberal professionals' (advocates, architects, land surveyors, teachers, etc) to work for a wage, but not improper for 'gratuitous' services rendered under a *mandatum* (mandate) to be 'rewarded' through gifts. But to *penalise* the reception of gifts above a certain sum would have meant, inconveniently, exposing prominent individuals to the adverse publicity of court proceedings. The legislator's choice to simply prohibit the relevant gifts entails, in practice, that gifts merely promised but not yet handed over cannot be judicially claimed. The law does not 'rescind' executed gifts, but it provides leeway for the praetor to block unexecuted ones. This the praetor will do, initially, by denying the donee the relevant claim (*actio*), and eventually (under the formulary procedure) by allowing the donor to raise a defence (*exceptio legis Cinciae*) when sued for payment. Here, one might say, the legislator prohibits, and only prohibits, because it cannot

---

23 In this spirit, Kaser, *Verbotsgesetze*, 33–9, jointly discussing, as *leges minus quam perfectae*, the *lex Furia Testamentaria* on legacies, laws that prohibit taking excessive interest, and the *lex Cincia's* prohibition of gift-taking by advocates.

24 My discussion of the *lex Cincia* draws on Kaser, *Verbotsgesetze*, 25–9; Zimmermann, *The Law of Obligations*, 479–82, 699; Buckland, *Roman Law*, 254–5; O Karlowa, *Der Römische Civilprozess zur Zeit der Legisactionen* (Berlin, Weidmannsche Buchhandlung, 1872) 348–9; Karlowa, *Römische Rechtsgeschichte I*, note 5 at 427–8; Puchta, *Institutionen*, vol I, 283–4.

(or must not) penalise, let alone rescind. The sheer prohibition, given its procedural bearing, yields effects that very much approximate those of a rescission, at least in some cases. As Puchta notes, the legislator is leaving it to the praetor, who is closer to the facts, to weed out lightheaded or precipitate gifts, the ones genuinely targeted by this legislative measure.[25]

Taken together, and on the basis of the above examples, the threefold distinction between kinds of *leges* is far from instantiating the now familiar contrast between prohibition and invalidity as more or less independent kinds of legal consequence with fundamentally different rationales. Rather, the two earlier modes of legislation ('imperfect laws' and 'laws that are short of perfect') in many ways operate as surrogate methods for rescinding – for reversing – a transaction.[26] Confirming the focally surrogate character of these earlier forms of legal curbing, an imperial constitution (decree) of 439 AD, known as the '*lex non dubium*' because it claims to state its rules for the avoidance of doubt, establishes that in the future it shall 'be sufficient' for the legislator to prohibit 'what he does not wish to be done', as a prohibition is to be construed as nullifying the relevant act, in the way of a *lex perfecta*.[27] Nullification is in truth the *more perfect* way of achieving what was once only achievable through penalties – which are mentioned no longer. We are still far, as will become clear in later chapters, from the medieval conception of some acts as being *both* prohibited (even sinful) *and* legally valid (chapter 5.III); and farther still from Suarez's careful disentanglement, *pace* the *lex non dubium*, of the intersecting ideas of prohibition and invalidity (chapter 8.II).

II. THE *IUS CIVILE* TIDE

The absence of a well-understood contrast between prohibition and 'rescission', and the presence, instead, of varying degrees of reversal of

---

25 Puchta, *Institutionen*, vol I, 283–4.

26 Other prominent examples of *leges perfectae* discussed in the sources concern manumissions (grants of freedom to slaves): they include the *lex Aelia Sentia* (4 AD), Ulpian's example, and the earlier *lex Fufia Caninia* (2 BC). It is in commenting on the former law that Gaius says that slaves manumitted in breach of the statutory prohibition 'will not be free' (Gaius, *Institutes*, 1, 46). Note that manumissions do not lend themselves to surrogate reversal through economic penalties in quite the same way as legacies and gifts.

27 *Code of Justinian* (Justinian, *Code*), [book] 1, [title] 14, [section] 5; '*[n]on dubium*' ('[t]here is no doubt that') are its first words.

transactions, strongly suggest that no robust, all-or-nothing idea of legal validity is in play in these regimes. So does the instability of the associated vocabulary. Our conclusions in this chapter, therefore, are mainly negative so far. Attributions of the idea of (in)validity to Roman lawyers, as found in some textbooks, are largely anachronistic. But we should not halt our analysis here. We have just surveyed some creative juristic strategies that are devised as ways to overcome or work around certain major constraints posed by the fundamental structure of the legal environment in which the jurists operate. In order to fully grasp what these strategies *and their imperfect success* reveal for our purposes, we should contemplate them in light of those very constraints. The constraints are, chiefly, (a) a deeply ingrained and only gradually eroding pull of *ius civile* principles of immutability and formality, and (b) a related conflict amongst the jurisdictions of the *ius civile* and the *ius honorarium*.

Notice how different a backdrop this is from the one that accompanies the use of validity in familiar contemporary legal systems. For one thing, our modern idea of validity attaches to things that can be done *and undone*, often by the author himself and, importantly, by the makers of other, systemically related, valid pronouncements (such as statutes) (chapter 2.II, feature (iv)). For another thing, our idea of validity attaches to things capable of *circulating* through many hands and in numerous contexts within one and the same legal system, without pervasively facing a clash amongst *internal* jurisdictions not amenable to being resolved by appeal to some higher-order 'constitutional' procedure or rule (chapter 2.II, feature (v)). The Roman legal order lacks a systemic arrangement of sources and demarcated fields of competence that would facilitate a cross-jurisdictional recognition of private transactions. Although transactions can be brought into the legal world, can be made, the ancient law does not provide for equivalent ways of cancelling them, and as these ways must be carved out of loopholes in, or be superadded onto, existing regulation, the ensuing miscellany of scenarios in which a transaction may be more or less effective gives rise, quite naturally, to a correspondingly haphazard vocabulary. Naturally as well, the ('valid') status that a transaction has in civil law, *and keeps* even in the face of more or less indirect attenuations through praetorian law, does not come to be expressed through a standard term either, uninformative as that term would be about the judicial fate of a claim, the primary concern of lawyers.

It is true that the *lex non dubium*, mentioned above, *does* give expression to the idea of a transaction's radical suppression. It provides that transactions falling under it are not only '*inutilia*' (useless) but 'must be deemed never to have existed' (*non solum inutilia, sed pro infectis etiam habeantur*). But this is the year 439 AD, and by now the fabric of rules that we know as Roman law has been substantially woven – indeed is at persistent risk of being transfigured, or deteriorated, by 'vulgar' modes of legal reasoning and learning that gnaw at a decaying Empire.

This should prompt us to appreciate the true significance of the juristic efforts at weaving that fabric of rules. The constraints of (a) immutability and (b) jurisdictional conflict are not simply obstacles to those efforts but *create the need* for them. Those patchy strategies for changing and discriminating the status of transactions in different predicaments embody the early stages of a technique that is as difficult to set up in this environment as it is required to handle expectations and claims. Roman legal thought lays the foundations of validity's craft precisely in working *towards* it, with the enhanced determination of him who has to sow rather than only water, to construct rather than just preserve.

III. CHANGING *OBLIGATIONES* BY SAYING SO

We can now take a step further, and track the close link between those efforts and other key developments that occur very much in parallel, and that we have touched on only in passing. They are not reflected in vocabulary associated to legal validity, but they bear on deeper aspects of validity's technique. They prove that Roman legal thought is genuinely incubating an all-round technique, not simply a way of naming the status of certain acts. Two developments are key in this context. The first one concerns the *way* one performs the acts of which the relevant status is predicated. The second one concerns what is ultimately *brought about* by acting in that way. Take them in turn.

The way in which Roman transactions are performed, at least from classical times, corresponds to the method that chapter 2 (section II, feature (ii)) has portrayed as the modus operandi of legal validity. Roman transactions are performed, in essence, *by so saying*. Roman jurists are not keen on theorising about elements common to (what we call) transactions, but such elements exist, and central to them is the fact that, in greater or lesser degree, transactions come into being through a *manifestation of intent to that effect*. Gaius' famous classification of causes of contractual obligation into *re* (by delivery of a thing), *verbis* (by words), *litteris* (by writing) and *consensus* (by consent)[28] must not obscure the fact that contracts of the first three kinds also have the nature of agreements even before informal agreements become generalised in post-classical Roman law. Thus the most important *real* contract, the loan for consumption (*mutuum*), requires at the very least an understanding about the purpose of the physical transfer,[29] and a *litteris* contract, in turn, is a written acknowledgement of debt in the form of an account-book entry by the creditor with the debtor's consent. Perhaps most importantly, the paradigmatic *verbal* contract, the all-purpose classical *stipulatio*, manifests the person's intent to become bound in the form of an oral answer to the question (posed by the future creditor) whether he promises to become so bound. It is of the essence of *stipulatio* that the answer matches the question, at the very least by repeating what we might today call the *operative* verb (to make a first person singular sentence): thus '*dari spondes? spondeo, dabis? dabo, promittis? promitto, fidepromittis? fidepromitto, fideiubes? fideiubeo, facies? faciam.*'[30] The fact that the Latin language would not allow a response in terms of an abstract 'yes' doubtless bolstered the important role played by the Roman *stipulatio* in shaping our legal technique of doing by saying.[31] Clear traces of this technique are likewise present in the kinds of transaction we discussed earlier. The main type of will in classical law, Gaius recounts, involves the testator uttering 'Thus as these things are written in these tablets and in this wax, I so *give*, so *bequeath*, so *make my will*.'[32] By the early Empire, manumissions take the form of either a testamentary disposition, a consented inscription in the census roll or a judicial declaration. And before gifts become transactions in their own right, *stipulatio* furnishes a channel to accommodate the promise of a gift.

---

28 Gaius, *Institutes*, 3, 89 (my translation relies on Whittuck and Poste, *Gai Institutiones*).

29 Justinian, *Digest*, 44, 7, 3, 1 (*animo dari et accipi, ut obligatio constituatur*); eventually Ulpian (Justinian, *Digest*, 2, 14, 1, 3) treats the idea of '*conventio*' (covenant) as a general one also underlying contracts made by delivery.

30 Gaius, *Institutes*, 3, 92 ('Dost thou solemnly promise that a thing shall be conveyed to me?' 'I do solemnly promise.' 'Wilt thou convey?' 'I will convey.' 'Dost thou pledge thy credit?' 'I pledge my credit.' 'Dost thou bid me trust thee as guarantor?' 'I bid thee trust me as guarantor.' 'Wilt thou perform?' 'I will perform.'; my translation relies on Whittuck and Poste, *Gai Institutiones*).

31 On this and other culturally significant features of *stipulatio*'s development, including its unhappy recasting under Justinian that probably hampered its influence on modern regimes, Zimmermann, *The Law of Obligations*, 68ff, 84–5, 546–8.

32 Gaius, *Institutes*, 2, 104, my emphasis (*Haec ita ut in his tabulis cebisque scripta sunt, ita* do *ita* lego *ita* testor).

Secondly, the things that Romans understand transactions to bring about, or change, are basically *obligationes*. The likely roots of the idea of '*obligatio*' provide a fascinating glimpse into what is surely a defining turn in the history of Western culture, perhaps of civilisation, and certainly of validity's technique.[33] Although such roots stretch back into a period so remote that much about it cannot be affirmed with certainty, it can credibly be surmised that *obligatio* descends in more or less direct line from a primitive strategy for managing and reining in private vengeance against wrongdoers, a strategy that involves the victim's (or his family's) seizure of the wrongdoer's person, if eventually through state-supervised formal proceedings (so-called *manus iniectio*) and subject to 'proportionate' rules (eg *lex talionis*). Gradually the victim's right to vengeance becomes redeemable in money, and now the wrongdoer or someone on his behalf is able to 'purchase' his freedom: payment *to avoid* vengeance. Until payment takes place, however, the wrongdoer remains a hostage, physically tied or bound – *ob ligatus*. This mechanism for, effectively, putting pressure on someone to perform, soon begins to be used to guarantee commitments *voluntarily* acquired. The mechanism transits, as it were, from the domain of delict to the domain of contract. Forms of transaction arise whereby a person subjects himself to that power of seizure should he fail to perform – typically, to repay a loan. This is the likely import of the archaic transaction known as *nexum*. And yet, curiously, debtors are not yet regarded as being, in actual fact, debtors. Through a mimic of the original delictual scenario, payment still operates as the means *to avoid* physical execution. One does not 'owe' payment, or anything else for that matter. One is liable to be executed – *unless*, that is, payment occurs.

Evincing nothing short of an intellectual tectonic shift, by the time of classical Roman law the idea that a person *owes* performance *to* another, for example repayment of borrowed money, has acquired sufficient independence from the sheer conditional prospect of execution as to be the (or a) primary connotation of the term '*obligatio*' as used by Gaius, and later even defined in Justinian's Institutes as a legal relationship (*iuris vinculum*).[34] No doubt one cannot simply translate the Roman

---

33 Helpful overviews of this development, cast in German-speaking literature in terms of the difference between *Haftung* and *Schuld*, can be found eg in Zimmermann, *The Law of Obligations*, 1–6, 82–3; M Kaser, *Das Römische Privatrecht I*, 132–8; J Iglesias, *Derecho Romano: Instituciones de Derecho Privado*, 6th edn (Barcelona, Ariel, 1972) 369–76.

34 Justinian, *Institutes*, 3, 13 pr.

'*obligatio*' into our current idea of obligation or duty, not least since in Roman legal materials '*obligatio*' may characterise the relationship between (what we call) duty-bearer and right-holder as viewed from either end: thus Gaius lists *obligationes* as a species of incorporeal things (*res incorporalis*) on a par with, for instance, rights *in rem* (real rights), thereby plainly envisaging that relationship from the viewpoint of the beneficiary, to whom *obligatio* is a valuable asset.[35] But in a very fundamental sense, by way of laying a seed that will later fully germinate, the step *from* understanding performance as a resort to avoid execution, *to* understanding execution as a punishment for failure to render a performance *owed*, the latter being, if incipiently, the *reason* for the execution – that step amounts to a recognition of what is owed or due, of the practical *need* to perform a determinate action for another's sake, as being very nearly a self-standing entity, abstracted from the facts that have occurred in the past and the facts that can be predicted to arrive in the future. It is a step that has clear echoes in Hartian and Kelsenian attacks on a Legal Realist 'bad-man' distortion of legal duty.[36] Only here, unlike in those modern theories, the step does not amount simply to a sounder conceptualisation of a settled legal category, but to something close to the category's very birth – a birth that, needless to say, goes hand in hand with other abstracting moves, including the detachment of certain rights *in rem* (such as servitudes) from the respective material objects.

It is no coincidence that the legal culture that begins to conceive of *obligatio* in this fashion is also a legal culture in which *obligationes* can be acquired and modified, increasingly, by so saying. The two developments, concerning *what* is brought about and the *way* it is, are hardly unrelated. Surely in early times, when ritual procedure was still regarded as itself the cause of the transaction's effect, the magical connotations of words and acts contributed to the understanding that some sort of invisible bond

---

35 Indeed, it is one of the items Gaius associates to the broader term '*ius*'; hence '*ius obligationes*' (Gaius, *Institutes*, 2, 14). Gaius' much-discussed underlying contrast of such '*iura*', as incorporeal things, *to* corporeal things, including *dominium* (what we call the right of ownership), may be a mark of the difference(s) between the Roman idea of '*ius*' and the modern concept and grammar of rights (on the latter's roots, J Finnis, *Natural Law and Natural Rights*, 2nd edn (Oxford, Oxford University Press, 2011) 206–10, 228, 423–4, 465–6; J Finnis, 'Aquinas on *jus* and Hart on Rights' (2002) 64 *Review of Politics* 407; and J Tasioulas, 'Justice, Equality, and Rights' in R Crisp (ed), *The Oxford Handbook of the History of Ethics* (Oxford, Oxford University Press, 2013)).

36 Hart, *The Concept of Law*, 39–40, 82ff, 136ff, 141ff; H Kelsen, *General Theory of Law and State*, A Wedberg (tr) (New York, Russell, 1945) 166ff.

was thereby being forged, in lieu of the original physical bond. Magic may well be the proximate ancestor of our idea of a change in normative positions (chapter 2.II, feature (i)). And although the invisible bond forged by classical transactions is no longer regarded as magical, the understanding of *obligatio* as a deeply personal, originally physical, bond between specific individuals is never altogether shaken off in Roman law. This is so much so that even mature Roman law maintains, fundamentally, what is called the privity of obligation, manifested in the absence of a general recognition of the institutions of agency, cession of rights and contracts in favour of third parties. Roman law incipiently conceives of obligations and changes therein, but it does not in general terms envisage the possibility of detaching, of cutting loose, normative changes from the originating transactions and parties. This is therefore an additional, third, obstacle to the legal circulation of transactions. Their legal circulation is hampered not only as between jurisdictions, but also as between persons.[37] In contemplation of the received regime, that is.

And as Roman lawyers ingeniously mastermind surrogate analogues to credit transfers and forms of agency so critical to a flowering economy, and in many other ways row against the tide of *ius civile* constraints, with *ius civile* oars, they fabricate novel mechanisms to change legal relations and to enforce and recognise them as changed, mechanisms which in their rudimentary import instantiate the building blocks, at the level of vocabulary and technique, of modern private law and legal validity's craft.

---

37 The call for their physical circulation in written documents is correspondingly weak during significant periods of Roman law; only in the course of the classical period, for example, does *stipulatio* gradually become a written promise (Zimmermann, *The Law of Obligations*, 69ff, 78ff).

CHAPTER 4
ROMAN LAW-MAKING
Power Usurped

The previous chapter's discussion of Roman private law has already touched on a few kinds of activities that lie at the immediate origin of Roman legal rules, especially in and before classical times. These activities include the decisions of legislative assemblies that result in *leges*, and the practice of praetors giving rise to the *ius honorarium* (praetorian law). This chapter traces the evolution of law-making activities, and in this sense legal sources, throughout the life of Roman law. The idea of 'law-making', for reasons that the previous chapter foreshadowed, and that will soon become clear, must here take a rather broad meaning. This chapter is concerned to identify forms of doings and sayings that give rise to legal rules in a *relatively* targeted way, and in this loose sense can be said to *make law*, as opposed to merely integrating and sustaining the diffuse patterns of custom and usage that many of the old Roman rules and institutions are bred in.[1] In fact, the most puzzling feature of the story that the present chapter tells is the virtual absence, during a substantial part of Roman history, of *genuinely* targeted techniques for making law, that is, of modes for creating and changing legal rules literally by saying so (chapter 2.II, feature (ii)). This entails that very much of Roman law is not made in the way that Roman transactions are made. For it is not made through the exercise of a power conferred by a governing legal framework that anticipates and determines what the relevant *saying* will legally *do* in being uttered.

This has an important historical explanation. Roman political history is marked by a succession of violent, or at least unregulated, 'constitutional' transformations. As different bodies struggle for law-making power, we often find the legal status of the winner's say-so recognised ex post rather than legitimated ex ante. Most of the law-making sources we will survey in this chapter involve doings and sayings that, when they were (first) performed, did not have the capacity, legally speaking, to modify legal relations, or to do so with general or enduring effect. They are law-making sources because they have come to be recognised as such. Their recognition is not associated to a stable vocabulary for naming their legal status. This is natural given that the recognition is fundamentally gradual. Jurists speak about the legal status of these sources especially when that status has undergone some change. Therefore these moments of change will also be the main stops in this chapter's itinerary. It charts how plebiscites acquire the status of *leges* (section I), *leges* are subject to the Senate's veto (section II), *ius honorarium* (praetorian law) is consolidated as a parallel source (section III), *senatusconsulta* become vehicles for imperial law-making (section IV), and imperial constitutions also in other ways exploit ancient procedure to make new law (section V).

Before we start we should briefly flag up the character of juristic literature. This is the body of literature to which we owe the primary testimony of the recognition of the above listed law-making sources. Roman jurists, of course, do not write in the voice of law-makers either. They write in the voice of scholars recording what certain unnamed others, on their part, happen to recognise as a law-making source. The place of jurists as key builders of Roman law is perhaps an extreme instance of doings and sayings giving

---

[1] The legal standing of custom is acknowledged in eg Ulpian, *Rules*, 1, 4, and Justinian, *Digest*, 1, 3, 32.

rise to legal rules through eventual recognition, not prior empowerment. For jurists influence the law for the most part through unofficial tasks of advice, interpretation, instruction and literary production. Only some jurists ever come to wield the legal power to issue binding responses to questions arising in a case (*ius respondendi*), and it is only after the age of the great classical jurists that their writings are 'confirmed', wholesale, by imperial legislation that does not consistently take account of the relative quality of the writings.[2] On the whole, therefore, juristic literature does not make law even in that *relatively* targeted way characteristic of the law-making sources it bears witness to.

I. LEGISLATION BY POPULAR ASSEMBLIES

Legislation by the Republican popular assemblies (*comitia*) is perhaps the gold standard of law-making from a Roman point of view. Law-making in later ages will steadily be compared to that original mode of legal creation.

Along with magistrates and the Senate, popular assemblies are a major institution in the Roman Republic, that is, the Roman city-state that emerges at the end of the sixth century BC and gives way to the Roman Empire in the first century BC. Popular assemblies are not representative: they comprise the whole relevant Roman population. They differ in the way in which the vote of different segments of that population is weighed. From the early Republic, the power to legislate, by giving *leges*, is primarily in the hands of the assembly known as *comitia centuriata*, which is effectively controlled by patricians (members of the nobility). Theirs is, for example, the Law of the Twelve Tables (450 BC), probably the first piece of promulgated Roman legislation. At that time, the populace (*plebs*), organised as a corporation since 494 BC, can only vote on decrees binding upon its own members. These decrees are known as plebiscites.

The legal status of plebiscites is changed by the *lex Hortensia* in 286 BC, itself an enactment of *comitia centuriata*. It provides, says Gaius, that plebiscites shall be binding upon (*tenerent*) the whole Roman people,

2 Valentinian III's 'law of citations' (426 AD) determines whose writings may be cited. It provides, oddly, that if jurists disagree one is to follow the majority, and that Papinian prevails if there is a tie. The Digest (533 AD), in turn, authoritatively collates an extravagant miscellany of juristic quotes of all ages (see chapter 5.I).

not only upon plebeians; prior to the *lex Hortensia*, he adds, patricians used to say that they were not bound by plebiscites (*se non teneri*), as they were made without their authority.[3] Through the *lex Hortensia*, Gaius concludes, plebiscites are put on a par with *leges* (*itaque eo modo legibus exaequata sunt*). According to Pomponius, although plebiscites and *leges* remain distinct in the way they are made (*species constituendi*), by virtue of the *lex Hortensia* their force is the same (*potestas autem eadem esset*).[4] After the *lex Hortensia*, plebiscites become the primary mode of law-making. The *lex Hortensia*, in a sense, is the first recorded positive conferral of law-making power.[5]

Let us briefly dwell on the nature of comitial *leges* as law-making sources. They instantiate the idea of popular sovereignty, an idea that, according to Mommsen, is inherent in the Roman political order from its inception.[6] At this early time, as probably never again in Roman history, the people are bound to the extent they have consented to be. It is significant that the *way* in which enactments are adopted unmistakably echoes the procedure of *stipulatio* (chapter 3.III). Technically, enactments are expressions of agreement by assembly members in direct answer to a question addressed to them by a magistrate (who is, in a broad sense, a legal official). Almost in the way of contracting partners, the magistrate makes an enquiry in the form '*vos rogo quirites*' (I ask you citizens) and the assembly responds '*uti rogas [, volo vel jubeo]*' (as you ask [, I will or order]) to give an unqualified yes. This is why comitial decisions approved in this manner, which renders more prominent the question than the answer, are called *rogationes*. Although the assembly does not have the initiative to legislate, it has the capacity to decide. It makes law, *leges rogatae*, effectively by so saying.

---

3 Gaius, *Institutes*, 1, 3.

4 Justinian, *Digest*, 1, 2, 2, 8.

5 As a preliminary to this conferral, the *leges Valeria et Horatiae Consulum* of 449 BC apparently bestow on *concilia plebis* the condition of *comitia*; when presided by patrician magistrates they are called *comitia tributa* and also have some legislative activity (PGH Willems, *Droit Public Romain ou Les Institutions Politiques de Rome depuis l'Origin de a Ville jusqu'a Justinian*, 5th edn (Louvain, Peeters, 1833) 165). On the possible general binding force of some plebiscites even before the *lex Hortensia*, see ibid 178–9; T Mommsen, *Römisches Staatsrecht*, vol III, part I (Leipzig, Hirzel, 1887) 155–60.

6 Mommsen, *Römisches Staatsrecht*, vol III, part I, 300ff.

II. SENATE'S VETO

The early mode of legal creation just outlined is accompanied by an imperfect but still remarkable set of mechanisms for legal checks amongst different public powers.[7] These mechanisms enable the Senate, in particular, to exert influence over the content of comitial legislation, even though officially it is only a consultative body. Among the different avenues open to the Senate for exerting its influence,[8] two mechanisms stand out as approximating early forms of review of legislation. Judging by the surviving evidence in mostly non-juristic literature, these mechanisms bring with them an embryonic body of systematic legal reasoning (chapter 2.II, feature (iv)), manifested in the understanding that the say-so of one kind of legal source may legally qualify or cancel the say-so of another kind of source.[9] The oldest of the two mechanisms is *patrum auctoritas*. It is a privilege of patrician members of the Senate. They, the elders, are to confirm the decisions of the people, not unlike tutors must confirm the decisions of minors (*tutoris auctoritas*). Such confirmation originally must come *after* the people's vote; the Senate can veto, and so effectively strike down, what the people have decided. Livius tells us that the people's laws are not established (*rat[ae]*) in the absence of *patrum auctoritas*.[10] Cicero says that a resolution that lacks the relevant approval should be considered null (*pro nihilo esse habendam*).[11] There were possibly no legal restrictions concerning the *grounds* of review, but in practice it would be (cast as) a check on the enactment's religious and constitutional permissibility.

In 339 BC the *lex Publilia* moves the *patres'* confirmation *before* the people's vote, so that the object of confirmation becomes the magistrate's

7 My discussion in this and the following paragraph mainly draws on Mommsen, *Römisches Staatsrecht*, vol III, part I, 363ff; T Mommsen, *Römisches Staatsrecht*, vol III, part II (Leipzig, Hirzel, 1888) 1037ff; Willems, *Droit Public Romain*, 178ff, 208ff.

8 For a comprehensive list, see Mommsen, *Römisches Staatsrecht*, vol III, part II, 1228ff.

9 It is a settled understanding that *leges* may in various ways modify earlier *leges*. This understanding finds expression in the specialised vocabulary of '*abrogare*', '*derogare*', '*obrogare*', and '*subrogare*', amongst others (Ulpian, *Rules*, 1, 3; Justinian, *Digest*, 50, 16, 102).

10 Livius, *Ab Urbe Condita Libri (History of Rome)*, book 1, chapter 17; in this sense also book 6, chapters 41–2.

11 Cicero, *De Domo Sua Ad Pontifices Oratio (De Domo)*, section 38; in this sense also Cicero, *De Re Publica*, book 2, section 25. Willems, reflecting on the sources, speaks of the *patres'* 'validation' of the vote (Willems, *Droit Public Romain*, 208).

rogatio rather than the vote itself.[12] Gradually this privilege becomes a mere formality, hand in hand with the loss of influence of patricians.[13] In the late Republic, however, the need arises for an occasional intervention by the Senate akin to the old *patrum auctoritas*, as there is otherwise no legal channel to control comitial decisions. And in turbulent times they are sometimes of doubtful legality. This second mechanism involves the Senate's check for, especially, defects of form, such as a disregard of auspices (*auspicia vitiata*). It is not entirely clear whether the Senate's review has a declarative or a properly invalidating effect, but the latter possibility is lent credence by several Ciceronian passages. Cicero reports that certain laws, passed through violence by radical tribunes, are no laws at all (*leges nullas putas*), having been removed (*sublatae*) in a single moment by a single word from the Senate.[14] He says that the actions of legislative assemblies can be rescinded (*rescindere*) on the basis of the judgement of augurs (who interpret auspices), and that *leges* can be removed if not lawfully passed (*legem si non iure rogata est tollere*).[15] He also explains that the Senate has abolished (*refixistis*) *leges* deemed to have been passed by violence and with disregard of auspices (*per vim et contra auspicia latas*).[16]

---

12 Livius, *History of Rome*, book 8, chapter 12; book 1, chapter 17.

13 As Mommsen (*Römisches Staatsrecht*, vol III, part II, 1043) explains, *patrum auctoritas* does not lose relevance merely in being moved before the vote. It had been conceived to protect patrician *Reservatrechte*, and the latter are vanishing hand in hand with the *Patriziat*. Mommsen thinks that plebiscites were never subject to *patrum auctoritas* (*Römisches Staatsrecht*, vol III, part I, 155, note 3); but according to Willems (*Droit Public Romain*, 180, 209) they were thus subject until the *lex Hortensia* (286 BC).

14 Cicero, *De Legibus Libri Tres (De Legibus)*, book 2, section 14 (as rendered in JEG Zetzel (ed), *Cicero: On the Commonwealth and on the Laws* (Cambridge: Cambridge University Press, 1999)).

15 Cicero, *De Legibus*, book 2, section 31; also Cicero, *De Domo*, section 40; conversely, one is said to have acted lawfully (*iure egisse*) if one has acted in accordance with the auspices (ibid 42).

16 Cicero, *Philippicae*, book 13, section 5. Sometimes, however, Cicero appears to claim in his own voice (ie quite independently of a Senate's decision to that effect) that the people is not bound (*populum non teneri*) by laws made violently and with disregard of auspices (eg ibid 12, 12; 5, 10, although here he goes on to stress the need for such laws to be rescinded by the Senate: ibid 5, 11); see further Mommsen, *Römisches Staatsrecht*, vol III, part I, 363ff; Willems, *Droit Public Romain*, 182 and 212. Other defects of *leges* noted by Cicero (in this connection) include missed promulgation deadlines (Cicero, *De Domo*, section 41) and disregard of the laws and usages of ancestors (*contra leges moremque maiorum*, ibid 68).

III. PRAETORIAN LAW

Comitial legislation coexists during the late Republic and the very early Principate (the first phase of the Empire) with the rise and consolidation of the *ius honorarium* or praetorian law. This body of legal rules grows out of a kind of activity that is about as far removed as it can be, in its technique, from the targeted enactment of general rules. Since the fourth century BC, the administration of the civil process is in the hands of magistrates known as praetors. With the introduction of the formulary (*per formulam*) procedure in 140 BC, praetors may grant claims (*actiones*) or defences (*exceptiones*) beyond those allowed by the *ius civile*. In their edicts, praetors outline the kinds of remedies they are individually prepared to grant during their tenure of office, which is limited to one year. A praetorian edict does not even have the status of a binding promise, never mind of a legislative disposition.[17] It announces rather than awards; what it announces is a procedural avenue rather than a change in substantive rules; and its scope is narrowly circumscribed in both space and time.

But aspiring praetors, no doubt following juristic advice, routinely incorporate in their edicts a corpus of announcements carried over from their predecessors. This is how praetorian innovative craft eventually attains enough homogeneity to warrant talk of a species of law, *ius praetorium* (or *honorarium*), existing alongside, indeed supplementing and correcting, *ius civile*.[18] *Ius civile* moulds need breaking, both in terms of the legal rules as such, as the previous chapter has shown, and perhaps also in terms of the subject making the rules: after all, Roman *comitia* no longer adequately represent the bulk of the population in an expanding Empire. Be that as it may, near the end of the Republic Cicero portrays *ius honorarium* as the main source of private law,[19] and, somewhat later, Ulpian refers to a given praetorian rule as a '*lex*' that does not derive from the sources of *ius civile*.[20]

---

17 The praetor is not in every respect bound by his own edict, especially after its one-year period of force has elapsed (Cicero speaks of a '*lex annua*': Cicero, *Orationes in Verrem*, part 2, book 1, section 109), although deviations from the announcement can trigger collegial intercession (ibid 2, 1, 119).

18 Justinian, *Digest*, 1, 1, 7, 1 (Papinian) (*ius praetorium est, quod praetors introduxerunt adiuvandi vel supplendi vel corrigendi iuris civilis gratia*).

19 Cicero, *De Legibus*, book 1, section 17 (written 54–1 BC).

20 Justinian, *Digest*, 38, 8, 1 pr and 1, 2 (Ulpian); the rule in question is *bonorum possessio*.

Ironically, praetorian law only achieves something close to the legal status of an enactment by the very move that deals the death blow to praetorian law-making. That move is the consolidation of praetorian edicts into one master edict, the *Edictum Perpetuum*, under Emperor Hadrian (130 AD). The text that effectively freezes *ius honorarium* is itself confirmed by a *senatusconsultum* (the source of law to be explained next). No fresh edicts may henceforth be issued.

IV. *SENATUSCONSULTA*

Despite its name, a *senatusconsultum* is at that time no more than a vessel for the Emperor's growing centralisation of power. It is an attractive vessel precisely because it has, by then, become the central form of legislation, largely superseding comitial *leges*. But, interestingly, the Roman Senate had never technically been conferred law-making power. Hence also it never technically loses it. Therefore, the rise and fall of *senatusconsulta* as sources of law provide fertile occasion for juristic taxonomical reflection and pronouncement.[21]

The Senate, as noted already, is officially a consultative body, although it has several channels to influence comitial legislation. *Senatusconsulta* probably originate as nonbinding requests to magistrates – hence the name. After the legislative power of *comitia* grows independent of the Senate in the course of the Republic, the late Republic once again places the Senate in the foreground. The other institutions, including *comitia*, are shattered by corruption and the upheavals of civil war. The Senate's say-so begins to be treated as occupying a place akin to that of earlier *leges*. Or so the jurists tell us. Gaius, halfway through the second century AD, lists *senatusconsulta* as sources of law immediately after *leges*, and notes that *senatusconsulta* have the status, or occupy the position, of *leges* (*leges vicem optinet*).[22] This point had formerly been controversial (*quamuis de ea re fuerit quaesitum*), he adds. As Pomponius recounts it, when the Senate stepped in to take care of the commonwealth, whatever it resolved upon was observed (*quidquid constituisset observabatur*), and this kind of law (*ius*) was called *senatusconsultum*.[23] The first recorded *senatusconsultum*

---

21 For a survey of this development, see WW Buckland, *A Text-Book of Roman Law from Augustus to Justinian* (Cambridge, Cambridge University Press, 1921) 13–5.

22 Gaius, *Institutes*, 1, 4.

23 Justinian, *Digest*, 1, 2, 2, 9.

that we can deem to have changed an existing *lex* stems from 10 AD; the last recorded comitial *lex* is dated 98 AD.

So *senatusconsulta* begin their career as legal sources by making law in the place of *leges*, *leges vicem*, and they end their career as cloaks for the Emperor's will – in that sense also by making law in the place of (*vicem*) something or someone else. The Emperor's gradual appropriation of the Senate has a significant reflection in the shifting legal relevance of the procedural steps involved in adopting a *senatusconsultum*. Already in the early Principate, Augustus (as *Princeps Senatus*) controls the proposals submitted to the Senate. The imperial *oratio*, the request for a decision of the Senate, soon begins to be cast in writing and treated as binding in its own right, that is, independently of its adoption by the Senate. Indeed, it is treated as binding the Senate *to adopt it*. Therefore jurists will often cite the *oratio* rather than the *senatusconsultum* as the relevant legal source.[24] The language of surviving *orationes* also captures this evolution. Under Hadrian they are still cast as requests, but under Septimius Severus they are cast as commands.[25] Eventually we find the writer recording the fact that the Emperor 'permits' the Senate (*permisit patribus*) to register the adopted resolution.[26] By now, the Emperor has other channels to make law, and these soon take over. The last recorded *senatusconsultum* is dated 276 AD. It is the end of a legislative institution that, as Mommsen puts it, never properly had, but only ever exercised, legislative power.[27]

V. IMPERIAL LAW

One might have expected that, as the Emperor is left as the sole law-maker, having halted the development of praetorian law and all but absorbed *senatusconsulta*, his say-so would operate legal changes through a most unblemished deployment of validity's technique – that, in other words, it would make law directly by so saying, using a procedure freshly devised to that end. But this does not quite happen. We find jurists discussing the

24 O Karlowa, *Römische Rechtsgeschichte I* (Leipzig, Veit und Comp, 1885) 643 (approximately from Hadrian's time).

25 Compare Justinian, *Digest*, 5, 3, 22 with *Digest*, 27, 9, 1, 2 (Karlowa, *Römische Rechtsgeschichte I*, 644).

26 Buckland, *Roman Law*, 15.

27 Mommsen, *Römisches Staatsrecht*, vol III, part II, 1237 (*Selbst unter dem Prinzipat hat der Senat die allgemeine Gesetzgebung mehr geübt als gehabt*).

legal status of the Emperor's law-making pronouncements, jointly called *constitutiones* (constitutions), in slightly careful and comparative language, similar to the language used with respect to *senatusconsulta*. According to Gaius, *constitutiones*, too, *legis vicem obtinent*.[28] And Ulpian writes that they have the force of *leges* (*legis habent vigorem*).[29] Only in another passage he says (or is made to say) that they *are leges* (*leges esse*).[30]

To understand the tentative tone of these juristic remarks, we must appreciate the nature and evolution of some early types of *constitutiones*.[31] They are strategies for the gradual centralisation of power by the *Princeps*, the early Emperor. At the start of the Principate, in the first century BC, it is still the Senate that formally makes law. But soon enough the *Princeps* claims the power to determine (*constituere*) and develop the law in doubtful cases.[32] *Edicta* (edicts) are a regular type of *constitutiones*. In *edicta*, the *Princeps* emulates the old praetorian announcements. He issues them in his capacity as chief magistrate. His *edicta*, like those of any magistrate, are binding over the territory and time span corresponding to his office tenure – it just so happens that the territory is the whole Empire and the time span is his whole life. Other early types of *constitutiones* are *decreta* (decrets) and *rescripta* (rescripts). They are issued for a particular case but eventually become binding on similar cases. *Decreta* include actual judicial decisions by the Emperor, whereas *rescripta* are answers to enquiries on points of law. It is no coincidence that the production of *rescripta* increases after Hadrian freezes the *ius honorarium* (130 AD). Here as well, the Emperor is stepping in, or trying to step in, as a developer of law in lieu of the praetor. In *rescripta* he replicates, as it were, the old praetorian formula, decisive for the case at hand.

Before long, however, the proliferation of precedent-setting determinations becomes problematic. Their juristic quality steadily declines, and there is

28 Gaius, *Institutes*, 1, 5, expressing no doubt about this (*Nec unquam dubitatum est, quin id legis vicem obtineat*).

29 Justinian, *Digest*, 1, 4, 1 pr (*Quod principi placuit, legis habet vigorem*).

30 Justinian, *Digest*, 1, 4, 1, 1; *Digest*, 1, 2, 2, 11 (*igitur constituto principe datum est ei ius, ut quod constituisset, ratum esset*).

31 The exposition in this paragraph and the next three relies on Karlowa, *Römische Rechtsgeschichte I*, 646ff (early Empire), 930ff (late Empire); M Kaser, *Römische Rechtsgeschichte*, 2nd edn (Göttingen, Vandenhoeck & Ruprecht, 1967) 150ff; and further Buckland, *Roman Law*, 16–21.

32 Karlowa, *Römische Rechtsgeschichte I*, 653.

growing conflict amongst them – not least since many are not issued with a view to being extended. Legal thought reacts by tracing some avenues to solve conflicts, evincing forms of systematic reasoning that may remind us of the time when the Senate could veto legislation. Thus Ulpian lists some kinds of *decreta* that are not to be deployed as precedent (*exemplum*).[33] And from Constantine (306–37 AD) onwards, imperial legislation *itself* circumscribes the legal force of certain *constitutiones*. Constantine, for one, provides that *rescripta 'non valeant'* if *'contra ius'*.[34] Rescripts can no longer change existing law.

Just as well, for it is now beyond doubt that the Emperor, the absolute ruler, can legislate at his pleasure. In this late period, which lies beyond the record of classical jurists, imperial laws are known as *generales constitutiones* (general constitutions) or *generales leges* (general laws). Although these provisions have the status of general enactments, still, remarkably, their legal *form* shows traces of non-legislative kinds of law-making, even of procedures that do not technically make law. Some *generales constitutiones* take the form of edicts. Although their force unambiguously extends beyond the issuer's lifetime, they never altogether lose certain formal praetorian marks. Other kinds of *generales constitutiones* take a form that has evolved from the old *oratio in senatu habita*. And yet others are technically addressed to the high official charged with enforcing and publicising them.

This enduring appeal of, and to, older procedures, even in the age of the Dominate (the late Empire), must be understood in the context of the period's conscious reverence of classical rules and institutions, of classical law. The old writings of jurists, along with imperial rescripts, are jointly referred to as *'ius'* or even *'ius vetus'* (old law), by contrast to new imperial *leges*. Legal production and science are in comparatively artless hands, and the dispersion of legal sources steadily worsens. This is the background against which, from the fifth century AD, legal collections and compilations seek to introduce, imperfectly, the systematicity that cannot or will not come forth by the contemporary legislator freshly so saying. We will pick up on this at the start of the next chapter.

---

33 Justinian, *Digest*, 1, 4, 1, 2.

34 *Codex Theodosianus*, book 1, title 2, section 2; provisions of similar nature by eg Arcadius (*Codex Theodosianus*, book 1, title 2, section 11), Valentinian III (*Code*, 1, 14, 3, 1), and Justinian (*Code*, 1, 14, 12 pr).

So the history of Roman law-making, not unlike the history of Roman transactions, is marked by a pervasive use of older legal forms to craft new legal realities. Whether for political or scientific reasons, Roman law-makers consistently place their point of reference in the past, and so do Roman jurists in accounting for legal sources. An interesting upshot of this is the emergence of the first signs of a generalising vocabulary in the field of law-making. From early times, new sources of law are compared to *leges*. Plebiscites are on a par with *leges*. *Senatusconsulta* occupy the place of *leges*. So do even imperial constitutions. While the original reference of '*leges*' was undoubtedly legislation by Republican *comitia*, one can appreciate an increasingly generic connotation of '*lex*' in the course of the developments this chapter has charted. '*Lex*' as a way of referring to a given praetorian rule, indeed to late imperial legislation, certainly no longer expresses a sheer *comparison* with a historically superseded kind of source, but rather an incipient *category* formed by abstraction from these and other sources, a category that these different sources *instantiate*. These may well be the stirrings of the idea of the legal validity of law-making acts, of legal enactments, although it will still be many centuries until this idea breaks through to juristic argument and language.

Part of the reason for this is tucked away in the normative universe of the Middle Ages.

CHAPTER 5

GRATIAN'S *DECRETUM* (MID-12TH)

A Novel Use

I. JUSTINIAN'S LEGACY

After the fall of the Western Roman Empire in 476, Roman law subsists only in a debased form in certain parts of Western Europe. In the East, it enjoys a revival under Justinian in the sixth century. The revival is fleeting, but it shapes the path of Western culture – half a millennium later.

The text at the core of this development is a compilation of Roman legal materials commissioned by Emperor Justinian. Originally meant as a restatement of imperial constitutions, it soon becomes part of a larger effort to restore and preserve the erstwhile greatness of classical Roman law and culture. The compilation is made up of four works.

The Code (529, 534) is a collection of imperial constitutions.[1] The Digest (533) is a collation of excerpts from juristic works, predominantly by classical writers. The Institutes (534) is a textbook of Roman law largely modelled on the homonymous earlier work of Gaius. What modern editions count as the fourth component work of the compilation, the Novels, is an unofficial collection of further constitutions, namely those issued by Justinian until his death in 565.

Justinian's compilation is hardly a competent achievement, considered either as a scholarly work or as a piece of legislative craft. Indeed, the compilation purports to be both a scholarly compendium and a positive enactment. It is devised not only as a repository of ideas past, but also as a blueprint of rules to govern the present. Perhaps because of the inevitable tension between these two aims, the compilation only imperfectly succeeds at either. Those compiling the text are awarded by Justinian ample freedom to condense and supplement material by way of weeding out what is 'obsolete'. The result, particularly in the case of the Digest, is an unsystematic assemblage of statements made by different jurists largely in isolation from one another, liberally edited in unattributed ways. It is certainly not the best of Roman legal thought that Justinian's compilation preserves.

But preserve it does. It saves the bulk of Roman rules that have come down to us from being entombed under the debris of a bygone civilisation. The manner in which this occurs could hardly have been anticipated by Justinian himself. Legal practice in Justinian's time is oblivious to his compilation, out of touch as it is with the local customary rules that have taken foot in many parts of Eastern Europe by the time the compilation appears. But Justinian's compilation spurs an unprecedented upsurge of Roman law study from the eleventh century onwards, at the dawn of an age of renewed intellectual drive (on which see further chapter 7.I). As it turns out, Justinian's compilation appeals to medieval legal thinkers because of the very features of the compilation that in a sense are its major shortcomings, and that deprive it of practical import at the time of its promulgation.

---

1 Restatements of constitutions had been put together in the previous century, first by private sources (*Codex Gregorianus* and *Codex Hermogenianus*), then by official ones (*Codex Theodosianus* of 438).

One of these features is the fact that the Digest forces into canonical written form juristic lines of reasoning that in their heyday had grown through fresh intellectual exchange. But it is just the book form that the medieval mind revers. Hence also the preferred scholarly method for engaging with Justinian's compilation in the twelfth and thirteenth centuries: the gloss. Glosses are marginal annotations on copies of the Justinian works. As generations of scholars contribute their marginalia, glosses add up to standardised bodies of text eventually studied alongside Justinian's 'primary' materials – 'primary', even though the texts only give (at best) second-hand testimony of juristic thought.

Medieval glosses typically record shorthand pointers to other passages in the vast compilation, by way of resolving conflicts and gaps. The profound lack of systematicity of the compilation is its second relevant feature. The scholars who come to be known as glossators are fascinated by the challenge to reconcile apparently clashing segments, and convinced that – as Justinian had declared – the Digest harbours no fundamental contradictions. They eagerly throw themselves into the task of retrieving Roman law, but in truth they do more than that. They construct partly novel systems of rules by creatively combining different building blocks out of the inexhaustible reservoir of ideas and cases yielded by Justinian's compilation, not despite its incongruity but precisely because of it.

And it so happens that the novel juristic projects that occupy the nascent forms of legal scholarship require, for reasons that will soon become clear, a grammar of concepts and techniques that transcends the horizons of local custom.[2] From a medieval point of view, Roman law is the law of the Empire. It is not local law but universal law: it governs all Christian peoples in the (known) world. This third relevant feature of the law enshrined in the compilation proves critical to the endeavours discussed in the next three chapters.

The most immediate project to which the fruits of the new study of Roman law are applied will be dealt with in this chapter and the next. It is the setup of the legal system of the first major state-like institution that unfolds in

2 And that also transcends the horizons of domain-specific orders, such as those governing rural, feudal or maritime relations (on domain-specific orders, see eg A Padoa-Schioppa, *A History of Law in Europe: From the Early Middle Ages to the Twentieth Century* (Cambridge, Cambridge University Press, 2017) chapter 13).

the politically dismembered medieval world: the Church. Canon (Church) lawyers introduce innovations in the technique of legal validity that pave the way for secular developments for centuries to come. Chapter 7, in turn, discusses the relevance of Roman law to the emergence of those quintessentially local, territorially bound entities that before long will blossom into sovereign states. We will see why, paradoxically, the Roman apparatus is key to sustaining an enterprise that by its very nature defies the lordship of the Emperor from which the Roman rules emanate.

II. GRATIAN'S INNOVATION

By the twelfth century, the law of the Church has reached a chaotic state.[3] Scripture, a millennium's worth of council and synod rulings from all over the Christian world, treatises of Church fathers, papal letters and decretals, sermons, even penitential manuals, and other writings, speak in overlapping and inconsistent ways to matters such as the status and rank of Church members, administrative and judicial procedure, Church property, and the conduction of sacraments and worship.[4] These sources are far from making up an integrated legal order.

In all likelihood, Gratian is a monk who teaches and researches at Bologna. Gratian, in a sense, seeks to unofficially replicate Justinian's task in the field of canon law. He writes a textbook to assist canon law learning and practice. Like Justinian, Gratian is faced with heterogeneous content stemming from heterogeneous sources, sources that do not flow from a single culture and were often not authoritative in their inception. Like Justinian, too, Gratian aims to attain systematicity in order to facilitate the actual application of these provisions. And although Gratian himself does not have the status

---

3 On the developments recounted in this section, see generally: JF Schulte, *Die Geschichte der Quellen und Literatur des Canonischen Rechts von Gratian bis auf die Gegenwart*, vol I (Stuttgart, Ferdinand Enke, 1875) 53ff, 92–107; A Keogh, 'The Codification of Canon Law' (1928) 10 *Journal of Comparative Legislation and International Law*, 3rd Series, 14; K Christensen, 'Introduction' in A Thompson, J Gordley and K Christensen, *Gratian: The Treatise on Laws with the Ordinary Gloss*, Studies in Medieval and Early Modern Canon Law, vol 2 (Washington, The Catholic University of America Press, 1993); P Landau, 'Gratian and the *Decretum Gratiani*' in W Hartmann and K Pennington (eds), *The History of Medieval Canon Law in the Classical Period, 1140–1234: From Gratian to the Decretals of Pope Gregory IX* (Washington, The Catholic University of America Press, 2008).

4 On Gratian's sources, see Christensen, 'Introduction', vii–xvii.

of a law-maker, already by the end of the twelfth century, a few decades after its appearance (estimated 1140), Gratian's text is treated as having authority in its own right. The *Decretum*, as the work comes to be called, is looked upon as an object of analysis quite independent of its sources. It, too, is eagerly glossed.

The rapid success of the *Decretum* is due to its innovative methodology. It goes much further than earlier collections of canon law materials, indeed than Justinian, in laying bare and harmonising normative inconsistencies in the source material. It is, one might say, *self-consciously systematic*; more so, at least, than its predecessors. That much is foreshadowed in the work's original title: *Concordia Discordantium Canonum*. In scholastic fashion, Gratian carefully works through any exposed discrepancies (discordances) in search for harmony (concord), which often enough he arrives at through a reasoned solution supplied in his own voice. Such *dicta* of Gratian accompany the statement of provisions along the *Decretum*'s three parts. The first and the third parts feature a range of texts organised around certain topics or distinctions (*distinctiones*). In the second part Gratian states a number of fictional cases (*causae*) and goes on to examine the legal questions (*quaestiones*) they give rise to.

Although Gratian's *Decretum* sets the cornerstone for the construction of a distinct canon legal system, Gratian himself heavily draws on the concepts and modes of reasoning of Roman law (scholarship), considered as the foundation of all legal science. Gratian's overall arrangement of the material arguably emulates the Roman sequence *persona*, *res*, *actiones* (persons, things, claims).[5] And in Roman style he devotes the opening section of the work, the first 20 *distinctiones*, to outlining the sources of law. That initial section amounts to a small treatise on law's nature, and contains the key passages for the purpose of appreciating the development of validity's technique.

These passages, as might be expected, evince broad continuity with the Roman building blocks of legal validity. But Gratian also refines those building blocks in remarkable ways. This is so *both* in the field of transactions and other individual legal changes, including the increasingly significant category of official or administrative acts, *and* in the field of law-making proper.

---

5 This is defended in Schulte, *Die Geschichte der Quellen*, vol I, 62–3.

III. VALIDITY OF TRANSACTIONS

The key development in the field of the validity of transactions comes to light, not unlike in Roman law, as legal thought ponders the status of transactions (and certain other acts) that have been performed in breach of a legal prohibition. Halfway through the work's opening section, a passage provides:

> You see, my dearest son, that what is accepted contrary to *leges* deserves to be dissolved [*dissolui*] through *leges*.[6]

This phrase broadly echoes the Roman *lex non dubium* (chapter 3.I–II). The *lex non dubium* provided that transactions contravening a law 'must be deemed never to have existed'; Gratian says that they deserve to be 'dissolved'. The verb *dissoluere* (to dissolve) does not, as such, connote a sharper idea of invalidity than the Roman *rescindere*, which Ulpian employed to characterise *leges perfectae* (chapter 3.I). As we saw, *leges perfectae* ('perfect laws') were not yet bound up with a robust idea of invalidity, comparable to our modern conception. The prohibition contained in a *lex perfecta* served itself to 'rescind', to invalidate, the transaction; it did not additionally carry a penalty. In Roman times, prohibition and 'rescission' were not genuinely distinct legal consequences.

Considered in isolation, the above passage of the *Decretum* does not suggest that legal thought has moved significantly beyond that phase. But the Ordinary Gloss to the term '*dissolui*' adds very important information. The Ordinary Gloss is the consolidated gloss that emerges as the comments of numerous glossators add up to a more or less standard text. The Ordinary Gloss to Gratian's *Decretum* may have come together some 75 years later.[7] One should bear in mind that, although glossators chiefly aim to clarify the text they comment on, they inevitably construe it through their own taxonomical lens, which presumably is that of their time – a time, in this case, of enhanced legal sophistication. Therefore, any moves we attribute to Gratian's *Decretum* on the strength of the elaborations in the Gloss must

6 Gratian, *Concordia Discordantium Canonum* (Gratian, *Decretum*), D. [Distinctio] 10, c. [capitulum] 10 (*Vides, fili carissime, quia quod contra leges accipitur, per leges dissolui meretur*). My translations of *distinctiones* 1–20 are based on A Thompson's translation in Thompson, Gordley and Christensen, *Gratian*.

7 Christensen, 'Introduction', x.

be understood as the fruits of an unfolding scholarly venture. (Of course, Gratian's *Decretum* itself is the product of an unfolding scholarly venture, being primarily a repository of quotes from earlier sources.)[8]

The Gloss to '*dissolui*' points out that the rule stated in the text (quoted above) is subject to numerous exceptions (*regula multas recipit instantias*). It goes on to cite three: contracting marriage after simple chastity vows, giving a judicial decision subject to a condition, and a bishop's consecrating a church within the jurisdiction of another bishop. In such cases, the marriage, the judicial decision and the consecration, says the Gloss, *hold* (*tenet*), despite the fact that they are contrary to law (*contra legem*), indeed prohibited (*prohibetur*).

This comment not only confirms that 'contrary to a *lex*', in the main text, means 'contrary to a legislative *prohibition*', and that this rule is indeed concerned with transactions and other particular acts-in-the-law – which is not apparent from the text's literal tenor. Much more importantly, the comment portrays, side by side, two different kinds of legal consequence as incumbent on one and the same act. The act is prohibited, but it nevertheless holds. Unlike with Roman *leges minus quam perfectae* ('laws that are short of perfect'), the act does not hold merely in the sense that it remains formally in existence under an archaic, increasingly superseded body of law. This is not a praetorian jurisdiction prohibiting and penalising a kind of transaction that it wishes to reverse, but that it cannot technically reverse under the system's older jurisdiction of *ius civile*. Here, in canon law, the jurisdiction that prohibits the act is the very same one – as Gratian's systematic zeal is keen to demonstrate – that also decrees that the act should hold *despite* its being prohibited. In the canon domain, prohibition carries a distinct import, closely associated to the idea of sin. And it is a central consideration in canon doctrine, as later scholars will emphasise, that prohibited transactions may or may not be dissolved: may or may not remain valid. The Gloss itself notes that canon law *does* dissolve marriages celebrated against a prohibition when there is a 'perpetual cause' for the prohibition: for example, a marriage between mother and son. In short: the three cases that the Gloss lists are *exceptions* to a coetaneous *rule*,

8 Indeed, even the text of the *Decretum* may have been put together by different scholars at different stages: see A Winroth, *The Making of Gratian's* Decretum, Cambridge Studies in Medieval Life and Thought, 4th Series (Cambridge, Cambridge University Press, 2004).

not imperfect or surrogate means to attain a partial reversal for want of a complete one.

That this reading is correct moreover follows from the nature of the relevant transactions. Marriages, in particular, do not lend themselves to partial reversal – not in the way that legacies and gifts do. A person either is or is not married, in contemplation of the Church. It would be most contrived to understand the idea of a marriage's 'dissolution', in the *Decretum*, as a condition that could admit of degrees as far as canon law is concerned, or be relative to particular jurisdictions within the canon order. Amongst other things, this could render a spouse who remarried guilty of bigamy. This kind of problem, incidentally, does not arise in Roman law, where marriage is a formless transaction with relatively little legal import. In medieval canon law, as in modern legal systems, marriage has fundamental implications of legal status. The binary, all-or-nothing character of legal validity is called for to handle this quandary (chapter 2.II, feature (v)).

It is not only the Gloss that works with the distinction between the prohibition and the (in)validity of a transaction. The *Decretum* itself reflects that distinction. The exceptions listed by the Gloss are exceptions that the glossator has found stated in other parts of the *Decretum*. The glossator simply draws attention to their existence. If we follow through the glossator's references, we will find that the relevant passages of the *Decretum* rely on that distinction, even though they do not always express it as precisely as the Gloss. With respect to a consecration made by the wrong bishop, for example, the *Decretum* says, rather openly, that although a bishop ought not to (*non debet*) consecrate a church that falls within another bishop's domain, in certain cases such consecration stays (*manente*).[9] And concerning a judgment wrongly given subject to condition, the *Decretum* conveys the fact that it remains valid through the phrase: 'but if it is [given subject to condition], what can you do?' (*sed si fuerit dicta, quid fiet?*).[10]

But the *Decretum*'s use of the distinction between prohibition and invalidity is not limited to the above set of passages. Here is another crucial set of passages that appeals to the distinction, which again is highlighted thanks

9 Gratian, *Decretum*, C. [Causa] 7, q. [quaestio] 1, c. [capitulum] 28.
10 Gratian, *Decretum*, C. 2, q. 6, c. 29.

to the cross-referencing task of the Gloss. This time the terms used are particularly significant:

> Because of the report of his complete lack of discipline … it is decreed that Maximus is not to be considered to have been bishop at any time, nor are those ordained by him to be so considered, because all acts done by or in conjunction with him have been revoked as invalid (*in irritum revocatis*).[11]

The Gloss to 'in conjunction with him', having clarified 'that everything done by those who have forced their way in or who have been defectively elected is nullified' (*totum cassatur*), points as confirmation to two passages of the *Decretum*'s second part. Those passages respectively use the term '*irritum*' ('*irritas iudicamus*', '*irritum erit*') in connection with transfers,[12] and the terms '*non valeat*' and '*cassabitur*' in connection with judgments.[13] The Gloss then flags up an exception to this rule in yet another passage of the *Decretum*. The exception is that, under certain circumstances, even a judgment issued by someone who ought not to have been a judge 'has the firmness of res judicata' (*rei iudicatae firmitatem tenet*).[14] The Gloss reconciles the exception with the rule as follows: 'acts are valid [*valent*] when this is to the advantage of the Church, but not otherwise'.

In light of these and the earlier passages, we can conclude that these lawyers have an idea of the legal status of transactions that is not only independent of the idea of prohibition (as the two categories may intersect), but also an all-or-nothing matter. That is the logic of the Christian marriage and of the provision that 'Maximus is not to be considered to have been bishop at any time' (in the spirit of the *lex non dubium*'s 'must be deemed never to have existed'). The last set of passages, moreover, reveals the timid presence of recurring labels to name that status, notably '*irritum*' and '*(non) valet*'. These terms appear elsewhere in the *Decretum* as well. In fact they are rather frequent. They characteristically qualify acts that are improper or faulty on quite a range of grounds, not necessarily linked to prohibition

---

11 Gratian, *Decretum*, D. 19, c. 10 (*Propter totius indisciplinationis eius doctrinam, … statutum est, ne Maximus fuisse aut esse iam putetur episcopus, neque hi, qui ab eo sunt ordinati, qualemcumque gradum clericatus obtineat; omnibus scilicet, quae circa eum, uel ab eo gesta sunt, in irritum revocatis*).

12 Gratian, *Decretum*, C. 12, q. 2, c. 37.

13 ibid C. 25, q. 1, c. 8.

14 ibid C. 3, q. 7, c. 1.

(chapter 2.II, feature (iii)): for example, elections to church offices made by princes,[15] procedural testimony given against a member of the Church hierarchy by a member of lower rank,[16] or consecrations, excommunications and other dispositions by persons external to the Church who thus lack the power to perform them (*potestatem non habet*).[17]

Plainly the terms '*irritum*' and '*(non) valet*' have now a more technical meaning than they did in many Roman writings, where they were just two amongst a wide range of terms rather unstably and unsystematically deployed. The verb '*valere*', in particular, can safely be assumed to have further lost its connotation of physical power, strength or good health. The increasingly settled distinction between prohibition and invalidity reveals an incipiently distinct legal technique, a way to do and undo things, and this technique slowly crystallises in a matching vocabulary (chapter 2.II, feature (vi)). But we should not overstate the degree of terminological abstraction. Although the verb '*valere*' has law-specific uses, the derived adjective '*validum*' and its negative '*invalidum*' are still primarily used in their original, non-technical sense: the Lord's word is '*validum*', strong and immutable;[18] one should pray for the '*invalidis*' (sickly);[19] and so on. And the derived noun '*valitudo*' consistently refers to a person's bodily condition or health.[20] The modern tags 'valid' and 'validity', the primary linguistic forms in our validity vocabulary, have not yet surfaced.

---

15 ibid D. 63, c. 7.

16 ibid C. 2, q. 7, c. 1; on testimony between orthodox and heretic persons, C. 2, q. 7, c. 26.

17 ibid C. 24, q. 1, c. 4. Excommunications that '*valet*': C. 6, q. 3, c. 3; C. 6, q. 3, c. 4. Other kinds of act said to be '*irrita*' or to '*(non) valet*' include ordinations (eg D. 71, c. 3), councils (eg D. 17, c. 5), marriages (eg C. 33 pr) and successions in office (eg C. 7, q. 1, c. 5).

18 Gratian, *Decretum*, C. 35, q. 10, c. 1 (*verbum Domini validum est et forte ... Est enim verbum Dei validum et forte, et durabile, et perseverabile, et inmutabile, non momentaneum, non transitorium*).

19 Gratian, *Decretum*, D. 95, c. 6 (*necesse est uisitare infirmos, orare pro invalidis*). Other non-technical uses, for example, in C. 33, q. 3 [*tractatus de poenitentia*], D. 2, c. 16 (*Qui uult facere Dei mandata, et non potest, iam quidem habet bonam uoluntatem, sed adhuc paruam et inualidam*); D. 47, c. 3 (*in carne validos habuit usus terrenae voluptatis*).

20 Eg in Gratian, *Decretum*, C. 7, q. 1, c. 15; D. 55, c. 12; C. 10, q. 1, c. 10 (*dictum post*); C. 7, q. 2 pr.

IV. VALIDITY OF ENACTMENTS

Let us now consider the *Decretum*'s idea of law-making. We left Roman lawyers as they began to use the word '*lex*' to designate enactments analogous to the old comitial *leges* (chapter 4.V). Gratian capitalises on this trend. Although at one point he records the narrow meaning of '*lex*' as the name for one kind of historical Roman source,[21] for the most part he stably deploys the term in a generic sense. This sense is given expression in an opening passage: '*Lex est constitutio scripta*'.[22] In Gratian, '*constitutio*' is also a generic term, equivalent to 'enactment'; there are both secular and ecclesiastic *constitutiones*.[23] So: *lex* is a written enactment. Specifically, '*leges humanae*' (human *leges*) are usages drawn up in writing and passed on as law (*iure conscripti et traditi*).[24] Of course the mere fact that rules are cast in writing does not entail that the written expression is what *renders* them legal as opposed to being the record of custom independently in force. But in the same section Gratian *contrasts leges* to usages (*moribus*) as species of '*ius*',[25] and somewhat later he says that '*leges* are instituted [*instituuntur*] when they are promulgated [*promulgantur*]'.[26] All of this, along with the very word '*constitutio*', of telling Roman roots, leaves little doubt that '*lex*' focally connotes a targeted manifestation of reflexive intent, a kind of doing by saying, as befits validity's technique (chapter 2.II, feature (ii)).

Three additional moves are symptomatic of the technique of legal validity. The first move is an enhanced concern with the *act* of enacting, perhaps as an unwitting by-product of the writer's concern with the person or institution

21 Namely law made 'by plebeians together with those greater by birth' (*Decretum*, D. 2, c. 1). Gratian is not clear about the relation between law emanating from historical Roman sources and '*lex*' in his generic sense; D. 1, c. 12 says that Roman law only binds Romans, but the Gloss suggests this might mean that it binds the whole world.

22 Gratian, *Decretum*, D. 1, c. 3.

23 ibid D. 3 pr.

24 ibid D. 1, c. 1.

25 ibid D. 1, c. 2.

26 ibid D. 4, c. 3. Such 'institution' upon 'promulgation' is different from the 'confirmation' (*confirmantur*) of *leges* by the usage of those who observe them (D. 4, c. 3), which usage, when contrary to *leges*, may even 'abrogate' them in what resembles the idea of *desuetude*. Other expressions related to usage and effects include '*viguit*' (being in force), '*robur proprium et vigorem*' (having its own strength and force) and '*hactenus inefficax habeatur*' (is so far to be considered of no force) (D. 10, c. 13; D. 19, c. 1).

issuing each particular kind of *lex*. The *Decretum* uses a range of verbs to that effect, including '*constituere*',[27] '*instituere*',[28] '*decernere*',[29] '*edicere*',[30] '*sancire*',[31] and '*promulgare*'.[32] Intriguingly, at one point it explains the fact that councils lack the capacity to enact law by saying that they are '*invalida ad … constituendum*',[33] in what might be a use of the adjective '*invalidum*' that is genuinely halfway between its original meaning and a law-specific, technical one.

The second move involves a dimly latent idea of a *transferable power* to make *leges*. But the passage in question refers to *leges* in the narrow, historical sense, the sense in which a *lex* is 'an enactment of the people' (*constitutio populi*) sanctioned 'by plebeians together with those greater by birth'.[34] The Gloss to 'people' (*populi*) clarifies that, while at one time the people made *leges*, they no longer do because they transferred (*transtulit*) this power (*potestatem*) to the Emperor. The writer of the Gloss even goes on to ponder the difference between a 'transfer' and a 'concession' of power.[35] Still, conferring power is not yet understood to be a separate function of laws, at least not at the time of the *Decretum*. The *Decretum* lists commanding, prohibiting, permitting and punishing as the only functions of *leges*, both secular and ecclesiastical,[36] echoing Modestinus' analogous passage in the Digest.[37]

The third move is an effort at working out some hierarchical relations amongst sources of law, which reveals an inchoate sense of their *systemic bearing* on one another (chapter 2.II, feature (iv)). Numerous passages of the early part of the *Decretum* stress, for instance, how natural law ranks

---

27 Eg in Gratian, *Decretum*, D. 1, c. 8 (*ius civile*); D. 2, c. 2 (plebiscites); D. 2, c. 4 (imperial laws).

28 ibid D. 4, c. 3.

29 ibid D. 2, c. 3 (*senatusconsulta*).

30 ibid D. 2, c. 4 (imperial laws).

31 ibid D. 2, c. 1 (comitial *leges*).

32 ibid D. 4, c. 3.

33 ibid D. 18 pr. The Gloss to '*constituendum*' uses the expression '*(non) potest statuere*'.

34 ibid D. 2, c. 1.

35 The latter term is used in Justinian's *Institutes* (1, 2, 6).

36 The quote at Gratian, *Decretum*, D. 3, c. 4 lists permission, prohibition and punishment, whereas Gratian's immediately preceding *dictum* lists command, prohibition and permission.

37 Justinian, *Digest*, 1, 3, 7 (Modestinus) (*Legis virtus haec est imperare vetare permittere punire*).

above both *leges* and custom, and how ecclesiastical laws in turn rank above secular ones (at least regarding spiritual matters). Such relationships amongst legal sources are mostly expressed in non-technical language that leaves open the important question concerning the legal status of the inferior rule when it conflicts with a higher-order one. Thus it is said that 'enactments ... yield [*cedat*] to natural law',[38] that 'both ecclesiastical and secular enactments are to be rejected entirely [*penitus sunt excludendae*] if they are contrary to natural law',[39] that 'enactments of princes do not stand above [*non est supra*] ecclesiastical enactments but are subordinate [*sed subtus*] to them',[40] or that rulers exceeding the bounds of heavenly dispositions will be offered 'insult' (*contumeliam*).[41] The *Decretum* claims both that '[l]aw [*ius*] is so called because it is just',[42] and that *leges* may well be evil.[43]

A few passages, however, do pronounce on the status of an inferior conflicting rule in comparatively more technical language. For instance: 'usages and enactments contrary to natural law are to be held null and void [*vana et irrita sunt habenda*]'.[44] Or: 'ecclesiastical laws cannot be dissolved [*dissolui*] by an imperial judgment'.[45] Or again: 'enactments contrary to the canons and decrees of the Roman bishops, or against good morals, are of no account [*nullius sunt momenti*]',[46] an idea that the Gloss casts in terms of derogation (*derogatur*) and removal (*tollere*). The clearest evidence we had found of analogous reasoning in Roman times, beyond the old Senate's

---

38 Gratian, *Decretum*, D. 9, c. 1 (*dictum ante*).
39 ibid D. 10, c. 10 (*dictum post*).
40 ibid D. 10 pr.
41 ibid D. 10, c. 3.
42 ibid D. 1, c. 2 (*Ius autem est dictum, quia iustum est*); '*ius*' includes *ius civile*, along with *ius naturale* and *ius gentium* (D. 1, c. 6).
43 Particularly in the secular domain: see especially Gratian, *Decretum*, D. 9, c. 1; customs and usages may likewise be evil (D. 8). He moreover insists that care is to be taken, in making *leges*, for them to be proper, just, in accord with nature, and otherwise sound, 'because after *leges* have been instituted, one will no longer be free to pass judgment on them; rather, one must pass judgment according to them' (D. 4, c. 2; D. 4, c. 3, *dictum ante*); also D. 4, c. 1 and *dictum ante* on the 'purpose' (*causa*) of *leges*. Gratian's wavering probably reflects the indeterminacy of the overall relationship between ecclesiastic and secular authority: the claim in D. 10, c. 4 that enactments contrary to ecclesiastical provisions '*nullius sunt momenti*' is extensively problematised in the accompanying Gloss (to '*constitutiones*'), also in light of D. 10, c. 8, which suggests a division of competences.
44 Gratian, *Decretum*, D. 8, c. 1.
45 ibid D. 10, c. 1 (*dictum ante*).
46 ibid D. 10, c. 4.

capacity to 'rescind' comitial *leges* (according to Cicero) (chapter 4.II), was perhaps the post-classical imperial provision that rescripts '*non valeant*' if '*contra ius*' (chapter 4.V). Now Gratian more self-consciously maps relations of source hierarchy, and, significantly, he does so in a language that he also deploys in the domain of transactions (eg '*irritus*', '*dissolui*').

This tenuously uncovers the important parallel in legal technique between acts that make transactions and acts that make law. This parallel is made prominent by canon legal thought about a century later, in what also in other ways represents a turning point in the development of the idea of validity in the West.

CHAPTER 6

THE *DECRETALS* (MID-13TH)

The Terminology Settles

I. THE POPE TAKES CHARGE

In the first official Church codification, known as the *Decretals* of Pope Gregory IX (1234),[1] we have found the earliest use of the modern vocabulary of legal validity. Still sporadic, but unmistakable. The adjective 'valid' (*validum*), the adverb 'validly' (*valide*), the verb 'to validate' (*validare*), indeed the noun 'validity' (*validitas*), are formed through an increasingly abstract use of Latin language, which matches an increasingly abstract grasp of legal technique (chapter 2.II, feature (vi)). Some of these

1 The text is also known as *Liber Extravagantium Decretalium* or *Liber Extra*.

uses, to be sure, appear in section summaries (*summaria*) that were probably added to the *Decretals* in the fourteenth and fifteenth centuries. So the development, as a whole, may be best thought of as a late medieval one. As the Middle Ages fade away, the tip of validity's iceberg, formed in the course of the preceding millennium, breaks through to the surface of legal terminology.

It is not by chance that this development occurs, or is palpable, in the context of an official codification. Both the method, the status and the scope of Gregory IX's code go to explain the prominence of legal validity in it.

Since Gratian's time, the production of canon law provisions has steadily grown.[2] Many of them are of papal origin. There is a need to organise this new, unfolding body of materials. But the *method* followed by Raymond de Penyafort, the Catalan friar whom Gregory IX entrusts the preparation of the code, is not limited to systematising existing provisions by copying their tenor. At the Pope's orders, he substantially compacts the material, eliminates conflicts and redundancies, and even turns provisions originally issued to settle particular cases into general laws. Gratian himself had *argued towards* general conclusions from provisions first devised to have a narrower import, but Gregory IX's code authoritatively *transforms* particular provisions into general ones – just by virtue of the fact that they are included therein.[3]

For the claimed legal *status* of the text is that of an official enactment. It is a code, not a textbook. It is not only concerned, as was Gratian's text, with correctly reflecting existing relations amongst legal sources or acts-in-the-law, but in important respects it *establishes* or confirms such relations in authoritative voice. Although, unlike modern-day codes,

---

2 The discussion in this paragraph and the next two draws on A Keogh, 'The Codification of Canon Law' (1928) 10 *Journal of Comparative Legislation and International Law*, 3rd Series, 14, 14–5; JF Schulte, *Die Geschichte der Quellen und Literatur des Canonischen Rechts von Gratian bis auf die Gegenwart*, vol I (Stuttgart, Ferdinand Enke, 1875) 92–107; JF Schulte, *Die Geschichte der Quellen und Literatur des Canonischen Rechts von Gratian bis auf die Gegenwart*, vol II (Stuttgart, Ferdinand Enke, 1877) 3ff, 25ff; K Pennington, 'Decretal Collections 1190–1234' in W Hartmann and K Pennington (eds), *The History of Medieval Canon Law in the Classical Period, 1140–1234: From Gratian to the Decretals of Pope Gregory IX* (Washington, The Catholic University of America Press, 2008).

3 See further Keogh, 'The Codification of Canon Law', 14–5.

Gregory IX's code records the original source of all the snippets it collates, the legal relevance of a provision does not depend upon when and by whom it was first decreed. There is no *lex prior* and *lex posterior* within the code. Legally speaking, all provisions date from the same day and derive their authority from that of Gregory IX's say-so (chapter 2.II, features (ii) and (iv)).[4] It is law about law: law regulating its own creation, as Kelsen would put it one day.[5] The code is not only systematic in what it portrays, but it is reflexive in what it *does*. It is therefore not only self-consciously systematic, like Gratian's work. It is self-consciously reflexive.

And its affirmed ability to create and change law has a wide *scope*. The code claims to cancel earlier papal decretals not included in it, and prohibits the use of any other canon law collection in court. (It does not purport to supersede Gratian's text, as the latter remains unofficial.) In fact, it has been credibly suggested that the primary motivation behind the code's enactment is not to provide a better arrangement of post-Gratian canon law, which has been well arranged already in collections published in the intervening years.[6] Instead the motivation, on this view, is precisely to demonstrate – to prove by actualising – the Pope's centralised power to freshly issue generally binding legislation on any point of law, even on matters traditionally regarded as falling within the remit of secular rule. These matters include wills and intestate succession, crimes and criminal procedure, and transactions involving Church members or otherwise bearing some link to the spiritual domain (for example because made

---

4 See further Schulte, *Die Geschichte der Quellen*, vol II, 16.

5 H Kelsen, *General Theory of Law and State*, A Wedberg (tr) (Cambridge, Harvard University Press, 1945) 124.

6 ibid 3–6. The first and perhaps most important of these is the *Breviarium Extravagantium* (dated between 1187 and 1191), an unofficial collection by Bernard of Pavia that breaks new ground in terms of its comprehensiveness and its coherent arrangement of subject matters into a (Roman-based) structure of books and titles. Four other major collections follow, two of which (of 1210 and 1226) are commissioned by the Pope. These collections, along with decades of scholarly work by so-called 'decretalists', significantly pave the way for the structure and content of the *Decretals*. On the influence of decretalists, see K Pennington, 'The Decretalists 1190 to 1234' in Hartmann and Pennington (eds), *The History of Medieval Canon Law*; K Pennington, 'Decretal Collections 1190–1234' in ibid; Keogh, 'The Codification of Canon Law', 15; Schulte, *Die Geschichte der Quellen*, vol II, 175ff. Although the work of decretalists must not eclipse the systematising task single-handedly undertaken by Raymond de Penyafort, it invites some caution in casting legal validity as a Catalan invention (alas!).

under oath or involving property in marriage).[7] Gratian would either sidestep such topics or defer to secular direction. A century later, canon law claims the power to determine them in ways incompatible with Roman law. It claims to be, to build up, a self-standing legal system.

This claim to self-sufficient law-making power crystallises in a new focus on the *acts* whereby legal positions are changed. It is these acts that are accounted for in the considerably (though not stably) technical vocabulary I have foreshadowed. A papacy in clear ascendancy takes control of its own law by deploying – and thereby developing – the technique of legal validity.

The novel emphasis on valid acts, indeed on acts that determine validity, is palpable both in the domain of transactions and in the domain of law-making proper. The *Decretals* treat these two domains in largely combined, even continuous, fashion, by contrast to earlier bodies of legal thought that tended to segregate them. That is yet another mark of the text's enhanced systematic concern. Our discussion in this chapter does therefore not separate the two domains either but focuses on what their joint treatment reveals about the consolidation of legal validity.

II. ACTS THAT DETERMINE VALIDITY

The development of legal validity in the *Decretals* is well represented by the phrase '*decernimus irritam et inanem*'. That is: 'we judge (resolve, determine) that it is null and void'. '*Irritum*' is a term familiar to us by now. It is used pervasively throughout the five Books of the *Decretals*, often interchangeably with expressions such as '*non potest*', '*non tenet*', '*ipso iure nulla*', '*cassare*' or '*revocare*'. But the frequent addition of '*decernimus*' or an equivalent verb (such as '*denunciamus*', '*decrevimus*' or '*revocaremus [in]*') makes explicit the act of bringing about or resolving on an act's invalidity.[8] An act does not just happen to be '*irritum*', but the latter is a condition that can be officially determined and pronounced on. The subject doing

7 For an extensive list of secular questions addressed by the *Decretals*, see the exposition in Schulte, *Die Geschichte der Quellen*, vol II, 25–6, concluding: 'One can say: there was no legal relationship, no aspect of social and also political life, that could not under some pretext be drawn into the competence of the *clerus*' (26).

8 Eg *Decretals of Pope Gregory IX* (Pope Gregory IX, *Decretals*), [book] 1, [title] 3, [chapter] 22; 1, 6, 18; 1, 6, 20; 1, 6, 38; 1, 6, 55; 2, 28, 55; 2, 28, 56.

the pronouncement ('*we* determine') is literally the author of the source text, and contextually and implicitly the code itself – hence Pope Gregory IX. The acts thus invalidated include elections, deliveries and injunctions. In short, we have one official act determining the validity of another act, which often is official as well. We have something like a chain of validation.

In order to appreciate how the new derivations of the verb '*valere*' come in to bolster this shift of emphasis, we should start by canvassing the *Decretals*' use of '*valere*' itself, principally in the long-established form '*(non) valet*'. This term is still recurrent in the *Decretals*, though not as pervasive as '*irritum*'. What is most significant is that '*non valet*' appears in numerous *summaria*, often as the opening words, across Books One, Two and Three. This helps to build up a sequence that resembles a hierarchical ordering of legal sources. Thus: '*Non valet constitutio*',[9] '*Non valet rescriptum*',[10] '*Non valet consuetudo*',[11] '*Non valet electio*',[12] '*Non valet pactum*',[13] '*Non valet sententia*',[14] '*Non valet compromissum*',[15] '*Non valet iuramentum*',[16] '*Non valet confirmatio*',[17] '*Non valet promissio*',[18] '*Non valet donatio*'.[19] The very fact that the term is used consistently, both in its frequency and location, is a mark of systematic awareness and suggests that it is a term of art. It also stresses the continuity between the domain of (private) transactions and the domain of law-making, although, of course, the law-making decisions whose validity is at issue are by subordinate bodies or officers within the Church hierarchy rather than by the Pope himself.[20] Even with this caveat in mind, it is remarkable that all kinds of decisions ranging from *constitutiones* (enactments) to *donationes* (gifts) are now said to be amenable to '*non valet*'. '*Constitutio*', incidentally, is just one amongst a group of terms that express a more or less generic idea of enactment;

---

9 ibid 1, 2, 6.
10 ibid 1, 3, 8; 1, 3, 10; 1, 3, 17; 1, 3, 26; 1, 3, 33.
11 ibid 1, 4, 3; 1, 4, 5; 1, 4, 10.
12 ibid 1, 6, 56.
13 ibid 1, 25, 4; 1, 25, 8.
14 ibid 1, 38, 2.
15 ibid 1, 43, 12.
16 ibid 2, 24, 2; 2, 24, 13; 2, 24, 19.
17 ibid 2, 30, 5.
18 ibid 3, 8, 13.
19 ibid 3, 24, 2.
20 For an overview of the relevant kinds of subordinate law-making bodies and the kinds of constraints on their law-making, see E Meier, *Die Rechtsbildung in Staat und Kirche* (Berlin, Georg Reimer, 1861) 118ff, 193ff, 211ff.

other terms are '*lex*' and the Church-specific '*canon*'.[21] The status-designating role of Gratian's term '*lex*' has now been taken over, at least in part, by '*valet*' as a term qualifying the relevant provision.

But the term-family of '*valere*' has grown. As specific passages of the *Decretum* attest, the verb '*valere*' has given rise to the adjective '*validum*', or rather its flipside '*invalidum*'. In Gratian's *Decretum*, it will be recalled, '*(in)validum*' was still used chiefly to denote physical strength or health (or lack thereof). Now it is the name for the quality or condition of something that '*(non) valet*'. The negation has become a prefix, transforming the simple denial of a state of affairs ('*non valet*') into the affirmation of a new, reverse, condition ('*invalidum*'). Therefore, acts are voided as invalid: '*tanquam invalidum irritarent*';[22] determined to be invalid: '*invalidam reputavimus*';[23] indeed invalid *ipso iure*: '*invalidum ipso iure*'.[24] Note the parallelism between the constructions '*irritam decernimus*'[25] and '*invalidam reputavimus*', and also between '*ipso iure nulla*'[26] and '*invalidum ipso iure*'.

So things can be *rendered* (in)valid and, what is more, a new dedicated verb captures *the action of so rendering them*. It is the verb '*(in)validare*': to (in)validate. The old verb, '*valere*', merely designated a state of affairs. The new verb designates a deliberate change in that state of affairs. In a revealing sentence, '*invalidare*' is used together with the matching adjective: '*Conventio invalida per consensum superioris validatur*'[27] – an invalid convention is validated by the consent of one's superior. '*(In)validare*' also appears at a strategic place, namely the *summarium* of the very first section of Book Four, on marriage: '*Matrimonium solo consensu contrahitur nec invalidatur si consuetudo patriae non servetur*'.[28] Marriage is contracted by mere consent; non-observance of regional marriage customs does not invalidate it.

21 See, significantly, Pope Gregory IX, *Decretals*, 1, 2, 1 and 3 under the common heading (*titulus*) '*De constitutionibus*'.
22 ibid 1, 6, 52.
23 ibid 1, 6, 54.
24 ibid 1, 2, 8.
25 ibid 2, 28, 55.
26 ibid 2, 28, 1.
27 ibid 1, 35, 2 (*summarium*); the *capitulum*'s main text speaks of '*ratihabitio*' (ratification) instead. The form '*ad invalidandum*' (for invalidating) appears twice in the *summarium* to 2, 19, 8.
28 Pope Gregory IX, *Decretals*, 4, 1, 1.

Quite apart from highlighting the human choice involved in settling legal validity, '*(in)validare*' brings to the fore another distinctive feature of validity's technique, when that verb is put in connection with the adjective '*(in)validum*' and the likewise new adverb '*valide*' (validly).[29] The feature is the *process–product* quality of legal validity, which we highlighted in chapter 2 (section II, feature (v)). Validity can be predicated both of an act and its result. One crafts a valid product if and only if one *validly* goes through the process. For it is the validity of the process that determines the validity of the product. Hence our familiar use of nominalised verbs (eg 'contract', 'judgment', 'resolution') to refer to valid products. Given the process–product quality of legal validity, targeted law-shaping choices can be referred to and engaged with later on, and by others, precisely as past choices and yet also as present objects, capable of circulating relatively independently of the circumstances of the original decision and the person making it.

The abstracting course manifested in the *Decretals* reaches its peak when a *noun* is used to label the property of being valid: '*validitas*'. It, too, surfaces in a *summarium* of Book One. The phrase specifies which judicial organ 'should determine the validity of an appeal': '*cognoscere debet de validitate appellationis*'.[30] Appeals are possible because of institutional hierarchy; some institutions can pronounce on the status of decisions by other agents; and the status which is the object of pronouncement is, itself, given a name: validity.

So here it is, an early glimpse of what will eventually become an all-purpose familiar tag with a corresponding currency-like use not yet evidenced in the *Decretals*. That there is more to legal validity than a linguistic pattern, that there is a technique of which '*validitas*' and its cognates are only a surface mark, is nicely illustrated in the *Decretals* by the curious fact that the status of marriages, a doctrinally central question to which a whole book of the *Decretals* is devoted, is scarcely discussed in the language of '*valere*' and '*irritum*' even though it raises problems that ostensibly involve an intersection between the concepts of prohibition and invalidity.

---

29 The *summarium* to Pope Gregory IX, *Decretals*, 1, 43, 4 speaks of '*valide compromitti*' (validly agreeing to an arbitration).

30 Pope Gregory IX, *Decretals*, 1, 3, 29 (*Si occasione duorum rescriptorum, unius scilicet in causa principali, alterius in causa appellationis, contenditur, non iudex super principali, sed deputatus super appellatione, cognoscere debet de validitate appellationis*).

The contrast between prohibitions that invalidate and prohibitions that do not was already hinted at in the *Decretum*'s treatment of marriages, as we saw. In the *Decretals* we find that contrast formalised in technical language – although that language is the marriage-specific one of '*impedire*' and '*dirimere*' (and '*dissolvere*').[31] A now robust legal technique is in play across diverse areas of the consolidating canon legal order. It is more deeply anchored than the surface vocabulary suggests.

And after this development there is no looking back. Canon law continues to unfold as a distinct legal system, a system in which, for centuries, the *Decretals* remain the only compilation that can strictly be called a code.[32] The canon legal order has emancipated from the secular one on the back of a claim to overriding law-making power. This is fundamentally unlike the way in which, say, the Roman *ius honorarium* carves a space for a new body of rules by way of supplementing, rather than supplanting, the old *ius civile*. The new canon law is generated through an exercise of the technique of validity.

Still, canon law's adoption of the technique of validity is constricted in one significant respect. There is hardly room for pondering the legal validity or invalidity of that generative law itself. That is because Pope's say-so is not legally open to question within the parameters of the canon legal order and the set of beliefs and assumptions informing it. As one might put it, at the apex of the canon legal order is a person, whose power derives from God rather than from a set of further strictly *legal* rules. Law-making in its primary expression is not yet regarded as liable to being valid or invalid. But it is not long before legal thought crosses that threshold.

---

31 This language is much more technical than the language in Gratian's *Decretum* and its Gloss. Compare, for example, the Gloss' elementary reference to the status of a marriage contracted after simple vows, which '*tenet*' despite being '*contra legem*' (Gloss to '*dissolui*' at Gratian, *Decretum*, D. 10, c. 10), to the *summarium* at Pope Gregory IX, *Decretals*, 4, 6, 3: '*Votum solenne impedit et dirimit matrimonium post contractum; votum simplex tantum impedit contrahendum, sed non dirimit post contractum*'.

32 The *Decretals* are soon supplemented by further collections. The first of these are the official collections known as the *Liber Sextus* (1298) and the *Clementinae* (1317). Along with the *Decretals*, Gratian's *Decretum*, and some private collections, they go to make up the *Corpus Juris Canonici* of 1580. It is not until the early twentieth century that a comprehensive, modern-style Code of Canon Law (1917) supersedes the earlier sources. For a summary of the development of canon law until the twentieth century, see Keogh, 'The Codification of Canon Law', 16ff.

CHAPTER 7
BARTOLUS (MID-14TH)
From a World State to a World of States

I. THE NEW PLACE OF LAW

We turn to the secular counterpart to the developments in canon law recounted in the last two chapters. The high and late Middle Ages are a critical juncture in the formation of political communities as we know them today. Central presuppositions of our legal understanding of the world, notably the idea of a territorially bound *jurisdiction*, acquire their modern contours at the hands of legal thinkers of this turbulent time. Legal validity, once again, has everything to do with it.

As noted in chapter 5 (section I), European legal scholars from the eleventh century onwards take an intense interest in Justinian's sixth-century compilation. In so doing, not only canon but also secular lawyers are motivated by practical concerns. The place of law in the communities wherein these scholars dwell is undergoing a deep transformation, on the back of a wider social and cultural transformation in the West.[1] Early medieval feudal relationships, largely regimented by oral standards and focused on personal and family status, gradually give way to the establishment of an urban and commercial class. Major cities are built, and new intellectual forms of labour gain independence from traditional manual forms of labour associated with rural life. In this dawning world of professional specialisation and educational zeal, specialisation in the ways of law becomes a prized skill. Young scholars flock to the schools that teach those ways. The first great law school is Bologna. It attracts brilliant minds from all over Europe. It is the birth of the modern university.

In this new European social environment there is a fresh demand for an artificial, *legal* grammar to mould social relations among persons not united by family, cast or regional ties, and possibly holding disparate views on the demands of justice – demands no longer reliably born witness to by a religious cast falling into disrepute. The Roman body of law, as contained in Justinian's compilation, is in principle apt to meet this demand. It has 'strongly urban connotations'.[2] It furnishes conceptual tools for mapping private exchanges and models of voluntary association that befit the character of the nascent social endeavours. And it is comprehensive, holding out solutions to countless sorts of substantive legal question – anything from the number of witnesses for a valid will, to the prescription of contractual debts, judicial procedure or the conditions for the sale of property shares.

In significant parts of Europe, however, it is not Roman law that we find settling such questions. What we find is 'local law'.[3] These are sets of rules made by and for political communities occupying circumscribed territories. Such territories may be large or small. To some extent they exist side by side – as in the case of adjoining cities or towns. To some extent they overlap – as in the case of a city and the kingdom to which it belongs. Law-making at the level of cities and towns, in particular, is an upshot of

---

1 For a helpful overview, see M Bellomo, *The Common Legal Past of Europe: 1000–1800*, LG Cochrane (tr), Studies in Medieval and Early Modern Canon Law, vol 4 (Washington DC, The Catholic University of America Press, 1995) 40–60.

2 Bellomo, *The Common Legal Past of Europe*, 58.

3 See generally Bellomo, *The Common Legal Past of Europe*, chapter 4; CNS Woolf, *Bartolus of Sassoferrato: His Position of Medieval Political Thought* (Cambridge, Cambridge University Press, 1913) 144ff; A Padoa-Schioppa, *A History of Law in Europe: From the Early Middle Ages to the Twentieth Century* (Cambridge, Cambridge University Press, 2017) chapters 13 and 14.

regional prosperity. It is the expression of a newly gained independence from larger, feudal political structures. Italian communes are an early and prime example. Here local legislative initiative yielding city statutes (*statuta*) soon becomes the predominant source of fresh production of law,[4] coexisting with custom (especially in rural areas), the laws of kings or other territorial lords, and particular bodies of precepts germane to some activity or cast (for example, feudal or maritime law).

Roman law – herein lies the difficulty – retains its place as the law of the Holy Roman Empire. Or so it does *from the Empire's point of view*. The Empire's claimed jurisdiction encompasses all Christian kingdoms in the known world. But just as the present Empire is a shadow of its ancient Roman predecessor, the substantive rules of Roman law are, in many European territories, at best a fallback regime resorted to *in the absence of* relevant local provisions. A growing number of communities, in Italy and beyond, self-organise as incipiently sovereign polities, 'city-states', which do not recognise a political superior – least of all an Emperor who is 'a German, seldom in Italy, and powerless in Rome itself'.[5]

Plainly, this fallback or residual role of substantive Roman rules cannot explain why generations of young men will travel from afar to go through a costly legal education whose curriculum features Roman *rather than* local law. (This is true about European law school curricula all the way to the eighteenth century!) Nor can it explain the blossoming of a dedicated industry for the reproduction of Justinian's texts.[6] The role of Roman law in late medieval legal practice is more fundamental than the above picture suggests. The intriguing relationship between Roman and local law harbours the key to the paramount developments of legal validity canvassed in this chapter.

And they are best appreciated in light of the writings of Bartolus of Saxoferrato, the jurist about whom later generations of lawyers will repeat *nemo iurista nisi bartolista* (no one can be a jurist unless he is a follower of Bartolus). Bartolus lives in Italy in the first half of the fourteenth century.

4 *Statuta* have their origin in the oath taken by communal officers, setting out the duties incumbent on them (Woolf, *Bartolus of Sassoferrato*, 146; Padoa-Schioppa, *A History of Law in Europe*, 177).

5 Woolf, *Bartolus of Sassoferrato*, 28.

6 On this scenario and the puzzles it poses, see Bellomo, *The Common Legal Past of Europe*, 63ff, 123ff.

By now the production of local law has consolidated, and the canon legal order has been set up along the lines described in the last two chapters. Bartolus is a lawyer and teacher of law. He writes on a wide range of legal subject matters. One of his most influential contributions is (what I will provisionally refer to as) a treatise on conflict of laws, a discipline that Bartolus, in a sense, inaugurates.[7] Bartolus sets out a series of rules for determining which body of local law, out of different potentially relevant ones, governs scenarios wherein parties and/or subject matters bear links to different cities.

Our interest lies not in Bartolus' conclusions about conflicts of laws, but in the arguments whereby he arrives at them. The question whether a given city statute extends to non-resident persons is not as such a question about that law's legal validity. It is a question about the scope of application of a valid law. However, tucked within the assumptions and structure of Bartolus' reasoning we will find a path-breaking application of the logic of validity, both in relation to private transactions and to laws proper.

II. VALIDITY OF TRANSACTIONS

For Bartolus, the validity of transactions is a routine juristic concern, which he stably expresses using the term-family '*valere*'. The following question about the validity of wills is the framing problem in one of the main sections of his conflict of laws treatise:

> Suppose there is a local statute or custom at Venice that a will is valid [*valeat*] if executed before [only] two or three witnesses: if some visitor has executed his will there, is it valid [*an valeat*]?[8]

---

7 '[P]robably on no topic has Bartolus received so much praise from modern authorities as for his systematic treatment of the "collisio statutorum"' (Woolf, *Bartolus of Sassoferrato*, 148). The more extensive version of Bartolus' conflict of law treatise is in Bartolus, *Commentaria in primam Codicis partem, ad Codex 1, 1, 1* (*Commentary to Code, 1, 1, 1*) ss. [sections] 13–51. A shorter and earlier version can be found in Bartolus, *Commentaria in primam Digesti veteris partem, ad Digestum 1, 3, 32* (*Commentary to Digest, 1, 3, 32*) ss. [sections] 25–31. Both versions (starting with the earlier one) are translated into English in JAC Smith, 'Bartolo on the Conflict of Laws' (1970) 14 *American Journal of Legal History* 157, 247. My own translations from these works of Bartolus are based on Smith's.

8 Bartolus, *Commentary to Code, 1, 1, 1*, s. 21 (*pone quòd statutum, vel consuetudo est Venetijs, quòd testamentum valeat coram duobus vel tribus testibus, quidam advena fecit ibi testamentum, an valeat?*).

The will is valid only if the local statute[9] extends to visitors; otherwise the will is invalid. We need not here trace the detail of Bartolus' discussion of whether it thus extends. The important thing for us to note, at this stage, is that local legislation, as Bartolus portrays it, speaks to the validity of wills. It sets conditions for wills to be valid, conditions such as the number of witnesses required. Elsewhere in the treatise, he refers to local legislation that also determines the validity of transactions in other ways: for example, by establishing other formalities for deeds or wills,[10] the procedure for emancipating one's child,[11] conditions for the valid sale of property shares,[12] a minor's (in)capacity to make a will,[13] or a man's ability to leave a legacy to his wife or otherwise dispose of his possessions.[14] These are all rules of a kind we find in contemporary private law regimes. They determine what we might jointly call 'criteria of legal validity'. They set conditions that, if not fulfilled, lead to an attempted transaction being null or defective.

It is significant that Bartolus groups these (otherwise very different) rules together when he draws up a general classification of rules in the framework of his treatise. That classification distinguishes between rules that are (a) prohibitive otherwise than criminally, (b) permissive, (c) punitive, and (d) concerned with the effect of criminal judgments.[15] The rules on the validity of transactions fall squarely within the first two categories, as Bartolus devises them. They respectively concern rules that (a) increase formalities, restrict capacity or otherwise limit what one may validly do, and are in this sense 'prohibitive', and rules that (b) decrease formalities, confer capacity or otherwise broaden the scope of valid action, and are in this sense 'permissive'.

---

9 Bartolus speaks indistinctly of statutes and custom ('whatever I may say about a custom is to be taken also as of local legislation and vice versa': *Commentary to Digest, 1, 3, 32*, s. 25) but, as an Italian scholar, he primarily has legislation in mind. The fact that he draws on French scholarship, where concern with custom is more prominent, helps explain his interchangeable reference to custom. I thank Kristin Boosfeld for clarification on point; see further sections IV and V of this chapter.

10 Bartolus, *Commentary to Code, 1, 1, 1*, s. 32; Bartolus, *Commentary to Digest, 1, 3, 32*, s. 31.

11 Bartolus, *Commentary to Code, 1, 1, 1*, s. 35.

12 Bartolus, *Commentary to Code, 1, 1, 1*, s. 32; Bartolus, *Commentary to Digest, 1, 3, 32*, s. 31.

13 Bartolus, *Commentary to Code, 1, 1, 1*, ss. 33, 38; Bartolus, *Commentary to Digest, 1, 3, 32*, s. 31.

14 Bartolus, *Commentary to Code, 1, 1, 1*, s. 33; Bartolus, *Commentary to Digest, 1, 3, 32*, s. 31.

15 Bartolus, *Commentary to Code, 1, 1, 1*, ss. 32, 44; Bartolus, *Commentary to Digest, 1, 3, 32*, s. 31.

It might seem troubling, even a mark of regression in legal thought, that Bartolus should speak of these rules as 'prohibitive' and 'permissive' rather than as disabling (invalidating) and enabling (validating). After all, we saw in chapter 3 (section I) how Roman lawyers cast as prohibitive certain laws that were in truth primarily meant to have an invalidating import: for example, laws prohibiting legacies that exceeded a certain amount. And we subsequently witnessed, in chapter 5 (section III), how Gratian and his followers incipiently disentangled the ideas of prohibition and invalidity: they argued, for example, that a prohibited (sinful) marriage may or may not be legally valid, thereby demonstrating that the ideas of prohibition and invalidity cut across one another.

But rather than showing disregard for a millennium's worth of scholarly evolution, Bartolus' discussion of validity-determining laws carries that evolution forward. Roman *leges minus quam perfectae* ('laws that are short of perfect') prohibited transactions as a proxy for invalidating them, at a time when it was not yet conceivable that fresh legislation could curb the validity of a transaction formally entered into following the principles of the old *ius civile*. *Leges minus quam perfectae* like the *lex Furia Testamentaria* 'sanctioned' the recipient of an excessive legacy to pay, *to the heir*, a 'penalty' of four times the excess of the statutory limit. Here, plausibly, the logic of punishable wrongdoing was used to engineer a surrogate rescission of the transaction. The 'prohibitive' laws that Bartolus groups under heading (a) have no comparable rationale. There is no doubt now that the legislator, here the local legislator, can set validity conditions for transactions. There is no punishment for breaching these conditions either. Bartolus even insists that some 'prohibitive' laws are aimed at protecting the person to whom they apply.[16] In his eyes it is not wrongful, never mind sinful, for a minor to fail to make a valid will.

For the whole point of Bartolus' fourfold classification is to *set apart* validity-determining laws *from* laws dealing with wrongdoing. The latter are captured under (c) and (d). That fundamental distinction is the very same one that early canon lawyers were at pains to highlight in stressing that sinfully celebrated marriages could, exceptionally, be valid. Bartolus relies on that distinction in a more overt manner. It yields the basis for a

[16] Bartolus, *Commentary to Code, 1, 1, 1*, ss. 32–3. Spouses are also subject to a similar 'benevolent' (*favorabilis*) prohibition to make legacies in each other's favour, lest they take advantage of each other. Note that here, unlike in Roman times, the 'prohibition' (limitation) of legacies is focally addressed to the testator, not the legatee.

key classification that gives structure to his treatise,[17] rather than (as in early canon law) emerging as an exception to a default rule contextually pointed up by glosses. Bartolus, to be sure, does not spell out the rationale for the distinction in the way that Suarez will eventually do, as we will see in chapter 8 (section II). But Bartolus' confident isolation of validity-determining laws is an unmistakable sign of legal thought's ever-sharper differentiation of the idea of (in)validity through its contrast to the idea of prohibition. The lingering terminology of 'prohibition' and 'permission' is therefore best regarded as reminiscent of Modestinus' classical division of the functions of law (chapter 5.II)[18] – a division that not even Suarez in the early seventeenth century has nominally shaken off.

There are three additional marks of the robustness of the idea of validity of transactions in Bartolus. First, Bartolus repeatedly discusses the making of valid transactions in terms of what someone can or has the power (*potest*) to do,[19] and says of this capacity or power that it is enhanced, even wholly conferred (*concessum*), by laws of type (b).[20] Thus, for example, a law that reduces the formalities required to make a will 'removes an obstacle' to the exercise of that power,[21] whereas a law determining the competence of a public notary to draw up deeds 'grants and permits something which in nature no one could be competent to do, but only by franchise particularly granted, and in matters to which it extends'.[22] As this last reference to public notaries illustrates, secondly, Bartolus deems exercises of private power to be relevantly similar to exercises of public power by legal officials deciding on particular cases. Thus laws governing the issuing of judgments,[23] notarial deeds and other acts of non-contentious jurisdiction, all fall

17 The distinction is also broadly echoed in another central classification Bartolus uses, which distinguishes laws concerning (a) contracts, (b) offences, (c) wills, and (d) other matters (mostly property) (Bartolus, *Commentary to Code, 1, 1, 1*, ss. 13–31; Bartolus, *Commentary to Digest, 1, 3, 32*, ss. 25–30). He uses this classification when discussing whether local laws apply to foreign *persons*, whereas he uses the classification I portray in the main text when discussing whether local laws have effects, or govern acts performed, in foreign *territory*. Each classification is meant to be exhaustive.

18 As 'commanding, prohibiting, permitting and punishing' (Justinian, *Digest*, 1, 3, 7) (see further chapter 8.II).

19 See eg Bartolus, *Commentary to Code, 1, 1, 1*, ss. 34–6, 23.

20 ibid s. 34.

21 ibid s. 36.

22 ibid s. 34. Bartolus goes as far as to suggest that, in the case of capacity-granting laws, it is the authority itself that performs the transaction (Bartolus, *Commentary to Code, 1, 1, 1*, s. 41).

23 Bartolus, *Commentary to Code, 1, 1, 1*, s. 41.

within Bartolus' category (b). [24] He even remarks that 'a testament is like a judgment',[25] invoking the claim in Justinian's Digest that 'a testament is the just judgement of our will'.[26] In so doing, Bartolus hints at the fact that both kinds of act involve a manifestation of intent (chapter 2.II, feature (ii)).

And thirdly, Bartolus openly reckons with the circulation of validly made transactions *across* jurisdictions (chapter 2.II, feature (v)). Roman lawyers had once inventively struggled to pin down the status of transactions in light of the unsettled relationship between the *ius civile* and the developing jurisdiction of the *ius honorarium* (chapter 3). Bartolus' world is also one of multiple jurisdictions, and he, too, struggles to render legal technique fit to navigate them. But the technique at his disposal is now vastly more sophisticated. Bartolus can take for granted that a valid transaction is apt to bear witness to a normative change beyond its originating circumstances and jurisdiction. It is this assumption that motivates his enquiry whether transactions made according to the laws of one city 'have effect' (*habeat effectum*) or 'have full faith and credit' (*faciam fidem*) outside of the city.[27] Some transactions do and some don't, he reasons. And in so reasoning, Bartolus, unlike his Roman counterparts, presupposes and vindicates that there is something conclusive to be said on this question *as a matter of law*.

This last observation points to a more profound dimension of Bartolus' argument. We have discussed Bartolus' misleading use of the notions of prohibition and permission *as opposed to* disability and ability. But no sooner is this puzzle unravelled than another one emerges. It concerns the classification of some laws as prohibitive *as opposed to* permissive, and vice versa (or, for that matter, as disabling *as opposed to* enabling, and vice versa). There is a benchmark inherent in the classification of any validity-determining law as either prohibitive or permissive. Go back to Bartolus' initial example of the Venetian law according to which a will made before two witnesses is valid. That law is permissive, says Bartolus,

---

24 ibid ss. 34–5. Bartolus even uses the same term, '*potestas*', in comparing legislative power and the power to make a will (Bartolus, *Commentary to Code, 1, 1, 1*, s. 23, also s. 37).

25 Bartolus, *Commentary to Code, 1, 1, 1*, s. 40 (*testamentum ... est quasi sententia*).

26 Justinian, *Digest*, 28, 1, 1 (*Testamentum est voluntatis nostrae iusta sententia*); my English translation is based on Smith, 'Bartolo on the Conflict of Laws', 253.

27 Bartolus, *Commentary to Code, 1, 1, 1*, s. 34, 35–6 (equivalent expressions in the following sections). Similarly, under rubric (d) Bartolus asks whether the effect of a (valid) criminal judgment extends outside its originating jurisdiction (Bartolus, *Commentary to Code, 1, 1, 1*, ss. 50–1).

because it reduces the formalities for a valid will. By the same token, for example, he classes as prohibitive a law that increases the minimum age for making a will.[28] In relation to what do these laws respectively *reduce* and *increase* requirements?

It is not an earlier regime within the same jurisdiction. Bartolus takes as his benchmark a regime that in an important sense *coexists* with the rules he is discussing – not unlike Roman lawyers did when they referred to certain laws as prohibitive or invalidating in light of the *ius civile*. Bartolus also invokes his benchmark when he says that some laws of type (b) enhance a *pre-existing power* rather than conferring a power afresh. They do the former when they concern private transactions. They do the latter when they regulate public acts by notaries and other novel professional figures. The latter are figures not as such contemplated by Roman law. As these observations should make clear, it is Roman law that serves as Bartolus' benchmark. It is in relation to Roman law that local law reduces or increases requirements.

Notice how this alone already suggests that, for Bartolus, Roman law is not a mere fallback substantive regime, liable to be displaced by region-specific regimes on point. Bartolus uses Roman law as his point of reference for drawing a *conceptual* distinction among classes of rules in a general legal treatise. Moreover, if Roman law were just a fallback regime, liable to be opted out of, it would hardly make sense for him to say that such local laws enhance a power *that is already there* by virtue of Roman law. Roman law somehow has a continuing relevance as a framework or foundational regime.

That much is clear, furthermore, from the very format of Bartolus' discussion. What I have so far been calling a 'treatise', because it is often so called, is in truth a small segment of his commentary to the Justinian corpus. Remarkably, the text that forms the blueprint of modern private international law is formally a part[29] of a commentary to the Gloss to the third word of the opening section of the Justinian Code, itself a collection of ancient imperial constitutions. That section begins with a reference to 'all peoples who are subject to our merciful sway …' (*Cunctos populos, quos clementiae nostrae regit temperamentum …*).[30] The word 'who' (*quos*)

---

28 Bartolus, *Commentary to Code, 1, 1, 1*, s. 33.

29 ibid ss. 13–51 out of 51.

30 Justinian, *Code*, 1, 1, 1 (based on the translation in Smith, 'Bartolo on the Conflict of Laws', 174).

is taken by glossators to imply that there are people who are not subject to the ruler. This prompts glossators to broach the problem of the scope of application of local laws.[31] To this gloss is appended Bartolus' treatise.

As a medieval legal scholar, it is Roman sources that Bartolus *annotates*. His notes do not take the form of scattered marginalia. Bartolus and his contemporaries and followers, known as commentators or post-glossators, draft substantial bodies of prose. Their commentaries reflect a greater concern to adapt Roman materials to the needs of the day. And yet such commentaries maintain their nature and justification as notes *to* a Roman passage. Bartolus argues in the voice of an authoritative doctrinal writer, like Gratian in his time and Roman jurists before. Indeed he consciously adds to an unfolding juristic venture, by offering to say what there is to be said, *legally speaking*, on the subject of conflicts of laws. Importantly, the body of law wherein he searches for the answers is not the local law of Perugia, the city-state in which he lives, or any other local law for that matter. His arguments on the scope of application of local laws systematically and exclusively rely on the authority of Roman and canon sources. It is not a local or jurisdiction-relative, but a universal conflict of laws doctrine that he sets out.[32] It is a Roman doctrine – a doctrine expressed in the grammar of Roman law.

This becomes crucial to grasping his position on the validity of local laws themselves.

III. THE DILEMMA CONCERNING ENACTMENTS

Bartolus' discussion of whether a foreigner's will made in Venice is valid continues as follows:

> On this question we must first consider whether the statute or custom is itself valid [*valeat*], and secondly whether, if valid [*valeat*], it applies to an outsider.[33]

---

31 The Gloss reads: 'Ground for the proposition that if proceedings are brought at Modena against a man from Bologna, judgment should not follow the local legislation of Modena to which he is not subject, since it says: "Who are subject to our merciful sway"' (based on the translation in Smith, 'Bartolo on the Conflict of Laws', 174).

32 Accordingly, for example, Bartolus argues that valid deeds or criminal judgments have effects *anywhere* outside the territory in which they originated (*Commentary to Code, 1, 1, 1*, ss. 35, 50).

33 Bartolus, *Commentary to Code, 1, 1, 1*, s. 21 (*Ex hoc themate, primò est videndum, an consuetudo vel statutum valeat: secundò si valeat, an locum habeat in forensi*).

The second question is the question of conflict of laws proper (to which Bartolus eventually gives a qualified affirmative answer).[34] Our interest lies in the first, preliminary question. Bartolus asks whether the local law is valid *itself*. Bartolus' neat disambiguation of the two questions demonstrates that, for him, the validity of local laws does not simply mean their scope of application or *validity-for-a-given-case*. Bartolus treats the first question (is the law valid?) as logically prior to the second (does it apply to foreigners?). His language is unambiguous as well.[35] He enquires about the validity of laws in the very same terms (*an … valeat*?) in which in the preceding sentence he has enquired about the validity of wills. By contrast, he consistently probes the scope of application of laws by asking whether they apply, extend or stretch to a given kind of case, never by asking whether they are valid (*valeant*) for that case.[36] None of this should come as a surprise, in light of his robust grasp of the validity of transactions and his incipient understanding of the transversal character of validity as applying to decisions public and private. His position is continuous with the trend manifested in the *Decretals* (chapter 6).

All this is confirmed in another seminal text of Bartolus, wherein he discusses some general questions about the status of local law that the conflict of laws treatise takes for granted.[37] That text is his commentary to another famous Digest passage, which in turn reproduces the opening words of Gaius' Institutes:

> The laws of every people governed by statutes and customs are partly peculiar to itself, partly common to all mankind.[38]

---

34 The statute extends to an outsider, unless in its terms it is restricted to citizens (Bartolus, *Commentary to Code, 1, 1, 1*, s. 24; Bartolus, *Commentary to Digest, 1, 3, 32*, s. 29).

35 He even uses the noun 'validity' in distinguishing a question of validity from a question of scope (Bartolus, *Commentary to Code, 1, 1, 1*, s. 38: *pro constanti, quod talia statuta valeant, alibi dicam, modo de ipsorum valore non dicam*). Bartolus uses the term '*valore*' instead of '*validitas*', albeit in just that sense, like Suarez (chapter 8).

36 The expressions he uses include '*porrigant effectum suum extra territorium*' (Bartolus, *Commentary to Code, 1, 1, 1*, ss. 32, also 13), '*an locum habeat in forensic*' (s. 21), and '*trahatur ad forensem*' (s. 24). He also recurrently (eg ss. 13, 18, 19) asks which law is to be looked to (*inspicit, spectari*).

37 Bartolus, *Commentaria in primam Digesti veteris partem, ad Digestum 1, 1, 9* (*Commentary to Digest, 1, 1, 9*) ss. [sections] 1–69.

38 Justinian, *Digest*, 1, 1, 9 (Gaius) (*Omnes populi, qui legibus et moribus reguntur, partim suo proprio, partim communi omnium hominum iure utuntur*) (my translation relies on EA Whittuck (ed) and E Poste (tr), *Gai Institutiones or Institutes of Roman Law by Gaius* (Oxford, Clarendon Press, 1904)).

For Bartolus, local law is that part of a people's law that is 'peculiar to itself'. About it he asks, in this order: (1) who can make local law,[39] (2) in what form,[40] (3) on what matters,[41] (4) to whom it applies,[42] (5) when it takes effect,[43] and (6) how it must be interpreted.[44] Only the first three headings concern questions about the *validity* of local law. It is no coincidence that these questions precede the *further* questions about scope of application, temporal effect and interpretation of laws already deemed valid.

Bartolus' understanding of local law as law 'peculiar to' a people, for the purposes of this passage, marks a shift from the passage's original reference. For Gaius and Justinian, the law peculiar to their people was the *ius civile*, and the law 'common to all mankind' was the law of peoples (the *ius gentium*).[45] When Bartolus speaks of law 'peculiar to' a people, by contrast, he does not have in mind the body of Roman law but bodies of law of more circumscribed territorial reach. The Roman lawyer focused on a single political entity whose head claimed to rule the world[46] – the focus was, so to speak, on a world state. The high medieval lawyer, instead, looks upon a horizon of emerging sovereign polities – the focus is now, so to speak, on a dawning world of states.

Naturally, this transformed political landscape pushes to the foreground a question that is as thorny as it is inescapable. It is the question about the bearing, if any, of Roman law on the validity of local laws.[47]

At first sight, it seems that anyone trying to answer this question will be trapped in a tragic dilemma, a choice between two unpalatable lines of

39 Bartolus, *Commentary to Digest, 1, 1, 9*, ss. 1–14.
40 ibid ss. 15–20.
41 ibid ss. 21–35.
42 ibid s. 36 (here Bartolus just points to his conflicts of laws discussion).
43 ibid ss. 37–53z.
44 ibid ss. 53a–69.
45 Gaius, *Institutes*, 1, 1 ('the rules constituted by natural reason for all [and] observed by all nations alike').
46 See eg Justinian, *Digest*, 14, 2, 9 (*Ego quidem mundi dominus*); on Bartolus' discussion on point, see Woolf, *Bartolus of Sassoferrato*, 21ff.
47 On the political stakes underlying this legal quibble, see Q Skinner, *The Foundations of Modern Political Thought*, vol I: The Renaissance (Cambridge, Cambridge University Press, 1997) 3–9. On the difference between (and recent scholarly confusion of) the question of the relation between local laws and the *ius commune*, and the question of the relative applicability of local laws themselves, see K Boosfeld, 'Die beiden Statutenlehren: Geschichte eines rechtshistorischen Missverständnisses' (2019) 136 *Zeitschrift der Savigny-Stiftung für Rechtsgeschichte: Germanistische Abteilung* 76.

answer. One line of answer available, it seems, is to say that the validity of local laws *does* depend upon Roman law and hence upon the say-so of the Roman Emperor as supreme ruler (chapter 4.V). But this flies in the face of the reality of the time: emerging Italian city-states act as politically independent communities rather than regions within the Empire's jurisdiction. The other line of answer, it seems, is to embrace this empirical reality and hold that the validity of local laws *does not* depend upon Roman law. The problem with this position is that it sits uneasily with legal scholarship's consistent demarcation of the jurisdiction of city-states *by appeal to Roman law* – the very law whose maker's authority the city-states hold in contempt.

Bartolus' stance is often portrayed as one that, in effect, grabs the second horn of the dilemma and sacrifices juristic rigour to faithfulness to fact. I will show that this extended reading of Bartolus is mistaken, although it harbours a core of good sense worth spelling out. Doing so, in the next section, will help us appreciate the full dimension of Bartolus' breakthrough in section V.

IV. THE VENETIAN STATUTE

In order to understand Bartolus' stance, we should look carefully at his discussion of the validity of the Venetian statute on wills. Given Bartolus' aims and primary audience (judges and practitioners), his engagement with particular pieces of legislation is more revealing on point than anything he can be found to say in the abstract in the text on the status of local law, taken in isolation.

The Venetian statute provides that a will is valid if it is made in front of at least two witnesses. It is a 'permissive' law because Roman law requires seven witnesses for a will.[48] But is it even possible for local legislation to override this requirement of Roman law? If so, why? In scholastic fashion, Bartolus first sets out reasons that others have put forward (or that might be put forward) for both denying and affirming that the statute is legally valid, and he then explains his own view.

---

48 Bartolus, *Commentary to Code, 1, 1, 1*, s. 36.

Bartolus considers two main reasons for denying that the Venetian law is valid. They can be summarised as follows:

(a) The first reason is that the law lacks the Emperor's consent – worse still, the Emperor explicitly disapproves of its terms: a passage in Justinian's Code provides that where seven witnesses cannot be found, no fewer than five witnesses shall be involved.[49]
(b) The second reason is that the law is 'bad and imprudent' because it facilitates forgery: various passages of the Code show that the requirement of seven witnesses was introduced to prevent forgery.

Bartolus then lists three reasons for affirming the law's validity, all of which are to the effect that the law *does* have the Emperor's consent after all. They boil down to this:

(a) The first reason is that, if the Emperor 'suffers' this law, he may be said to have established it: three passages in the Digest chart scenarios in which someone is deemed to have consented by acquiescence.
(b) The second reason is that the Emperor could have expressly granted this privilege to a particular city: the Code provides as much in relation to testamentary regulations.
(c) The third reason is that such privilege may equally accrue through a deep-seated custom: in two passages of Gratian's *Decretum* it is established that ancient customs can become law.

When Bartolus eventually announces his own view, he does so in no uncertain terms: 'As I see it myself, the [law is] valid even if the Emperor knows nothing of [it]'.[50] He offers five reasons:

(a) The first reason is that, in the analogous case of probate, which is likewise essential to the validity of a will, formalities may be reduced by local legislation compatibly with Roman law: the Digest and the Code provide as much.[51]
(b) The second reason is that a father may dispose as between his children in front of just two witnesses compatibly with Roman law, and in a

49 Justinian, *Code*, 6, 23, 31, 3.
50 Bartolus, *Commentary to Digest, 1, 3, 32*, s. 28; Bartolus, *Commentary to Code, 1, 1, 1*, s. 23 (*Ego credo quod statutum … valeat, etiam principe ignorante*).
51 Bartolus, *Commentary to Code, 1, 1, 1*, s. 23; Bartolus, *Commentary to Digest, 1, 3, 32*, s. 28.

number of ways the fatherland's powers to dispose in respect of its subjects are on the same footing as a father's powers to dispose in respect of his children: the Digest and the Code provide as much.[52]

(c) The third reason is that Roman law explicitly authorises the passing of local legislation: the Digest provides as much (in the passage quoted above, on law 'peculiar to' a people).[53]

(d) The fourth reason is that the Emperor's injunction against laws that permit fewer than five witnesses must be understood as applying only to laws already in existence, rather than to future ones: this is the view of Bartolus' master (another commentator).[54]

(e) The fifth reason is that the Venetian law is good rather than bad, because it prevents the frustration of last wills: 'in the city of Venice, on account of the claims of business, witnesses are almost impossible to find'.[55]

There can be no denial that the preceding body of argumentative moves, taken as a whole, is not entirely happy as a piece of juristic reasoning. For one thing, the Emperor's injunction against the use of fewer than five witnesses is unqualified. Justinian provides: 'We do not, under any circumstances, permit a smaller number [of witnesses than five] to be sufficient'.[56] The context of the injunction is that Justinian 'grants' that some wills may be valid with five rather than seven witnesses 'in those places in which educated men are rarely found', provided that their 'ancient' rural customs so provide.[57] By contrast, where 'the science of letters flourishes', as in urban settings, the standard provisions on wills 'shall be observed' unchanged.[58] The case for exempting Venice is tenuous. So is, for another thing, Bartolus' claim that the injunction only catches existing laws and does not extend to new ones.[59] This ignores the law's temporal logic.

52 Bartolus, *Commentary to Code, 1, 1, 1*, s. 23; Bartolus, *Commentary to Digest, 1, 3, 32*, s. 28.

53 Bartolus, *Commentary to Code, 1, 1, 1*, s. 23.

54 Bartolus, *Commentary to Code, 1, 1, 1*, s. 23; Bartolus, *Commentary to Digest, 1, 3, 32*, s. 28.

55 Bartolus, *Commentary to Digest, 1, 3, 32*, s. 28; Bartolus, *Commentary to Code, 1, 1, 1*, s. 23.

56 Justinian, *Code*, 6, 23, 31, 3.

57 ibid 6, 23, 31, 2.

58 ibid 6, 23, 31, 1.

59 Glossators and commentators would sometimes allow that custom could override earlier general legislation, but not an express legislative prohibition of contrary customs (S Brie, *Die Lehre vom Gewohnheitsrecht: Eine historisch-dogmatische Untersuchung, Erster Teil: Geschichtliche Grundlegung* (Breslau, von M & H Marcus, 1899) 120ff, 157ff).

A similar difficulty, not exposed by Bartolus, afflicts the view that the Emperor is 'suffering' the Venetian law – having unambiguously pronounced against it in an injunction not validly repealed. Indeed, *pace* Bartolus, the fact that the Emperor could have expressly granted an exemption to Venice, *but has not*, tells against rather than in favour of the law's legal validity.

In light of this, it is tempting to regard Bartolus as playing fast and loose with legal reasoning in order to arrive at a conclusion amenable to the legal practice of his day. This corresponds to the general diagnosis of Bartolus' political thought offered in Woolf's leading study. The study concludes that 'his object, unlike that of the Glossators, was to evolve from his texts a law rather practically acceptable than scientifically correct'.[60] In the opening pages of that study, we are told that the 'distinction between right and fact … is at the basis of all the political theories of Bartolus'.[61] Other modern writers follow suit. Canning calls Bartolus' position on the validity of local statutes 'a classic *de facto* theory'.[62] According to Waldron, '[t]he key to Bartolus' contribution … lay in his recognition that when legal doctrine appears to contradict stable and well-established facts, it is sometimes the legal doctrine not the facts that ought to be modified'.[63] And, in Skinner's view, Bartolus 'made it his basic precept that, where the law and the facts collide, it is the law which must be brought into conformity with the facts'.[64]

These authors are correct that Bartolus recurrently appeals to factual reality in support of legal propositions he advances. Chief among these propositions, for our purposes, is the proposition that an independent city-state has a capacity to make law, for its territory, akin to the capacity of the Emperor to make law for the entire world.[65] This is a striking

60 Woolf, *Bartolus of Sassoferrato*, 387.

61 ibid 22.

62 J Canning, *The Political Thought of Baldus de Ubaldis* (Cambridge, Cambridge University Press, 1987) 97.

63 J Waldron, *Law and Disagreement* (Oxford, Oxford University Press, 1999) 63.

64 Skinner, *The Foundations of Modern Political Thought*, 9 (approvingly relying on Woolf, *Bartolus of Sassoferrato*, 5); also 10 ('his basic axiom that the law must yield to the facts').

65 Bartolus, *Commentary to Digest, 1, 1, 9*, ss. 3–4; and elsewhere: see Woolf, *Bartolus of Sassoferrato*, 154–60. For simplicity I use the idea of 'independence' instead of Bartolus' more complex idea of '*merum et mixtum imperium*' (on the subtleties of the latter, which do not bear on my argument, see Woolf, *Bartolus of Sassoferrato*, 405 in light of 127ff).

proposition for Bartolus to defend and is deservedly famous. Bartolus goes as far as to say that an independent city is a free people (*populus liber*) that can make law as it pleases (*prout sibi placet*) within its territorial bounds.[66] Indeed, the city is its own emperor (*civitas sibi princeps*).[67] But *under what conditions* is a city thus independent? Here Bartolus' argument is sloppy. He recognises that a city's independence would have to be granted or consented to by the Emperor. But failing explicit imperial consent, he says, cities can demonstrate that they have acquired independence by prescription, or else by usurpation.[68] Particularly this last concession amounts to saying that they are independent in law because they are independent in fact.[69] 'This seems a rather lame conclusion', Woolf writes, '[b]ut in truth it is a fine example of Bartolus' aim and method, of his absolute adherence to fact.'[70]

Canning and Waldron elaborate on what they take to be the decisive *fact* in this context: the 'consent' of the people in law-making.[71] These authors read Bartolus as arguing for the legislative capacity of city-states through an analogy with custom. Bartolus – we are told – takes for granted that communities can create any customary law without superior authorisation. Seeing as legislated law is relevantly similar to customary law, in that both are made through the people's consent (express and tacit, respectively), Bartolus concludes – on this reading – that 'the law-making activities of the people, whatever the *de iure* claims of the emperor, break through to sovereignty'.[72] Or, in the words of Ullmann, on whom Waldron relies: 'the popular will [is] the reason for the validity of the law'.[73]

---

66 See Woolf, *Bartolus of Sassoferrato*, 154 (quoting from Bartolus' *Commentary to Code, 10, 63, 5*) and generally 45ff, 149ff; see also Bartolus, *Commentary to Digest, 1, 1, 9*, ss. 21–5.

67 See eg Woolf, *Bartolus of Sassoferrato*, 156 (quoting from Bartolus' *Commentary to Digest, 4, 4, 3*: *Civitates tamen quae principem non recognoscunt in dominum et sic earum populus liber est ... possent hoc forte statuere, quia ipsamet civitas sibi princeps est*). Towns and cities with more limited jurisdiction, by contrast, require the consent of their superior in order to validly pass certain laws (Bartolus, *Commentary to Digest, 1, 1, 9*, ss. 3ff).

68 Woolf, *Bartolus of Sassoferrato*, 122ff, summary at 144.

69 In a similar vein, Bartolus argues that the Emperor de jure rules over the whole world, but de facto only rules over the people that do recognise his lordship (Bartolus, *Commentary to Code, 1, 1, 1*, s. 1).

70 Woolf, *Bartolus of Sassoferrato*, 136.

71 Canning, *The Political Thought of Baldus de Ubaldis*, 93ff, especially 95–7; Waldron, *Law and Disagreement*, 63–5.

72 Canning, *The Political Thought of Baldus de Ubaldis*, 97.

73 W Ullmann, *Principles of Government and Politics in the Middle Ages* (New York, Routledge, 2010) 200 (also ibid, 'it is the will of the people which imparts binding,

Bartolus' reasoning on the validity of the Venetian statute seems consistent with these general assessments of Bartolus' thought. That reasoning similarly started by considering the need for imperial consent – here to a single statute that contradicts Roman law – and ended up dismissing this need. We know that, as a matter of fact, Italian *statuta* were often paid heed to in legal practice quite independently of their 'confirmation' by a political superior; a study of the region of Florence, for example, points out that a backlog of legislation pending 'confirmation' would sometimes accrue as the process turned into a formality demanded periodically for a tax, regardless of changes in the legislation.[74] So, in sidestepping his predecessors' dubious attempts to conjure up evidence of imperial consent, and boldly declaring the statute to be valid 'even if the Emperor knows nothing of [it]', Bartolus might indeed appear be vindicating the statute's legal validity on the basis of the sheer fact of its enactment – a fact that takes the place occupied in earlier legal thought by the consent of the Emperor.

But note what this position on statutory validity entails. If Bartolus is committed to the view that the sheer say-so of the people is (as Canning puts it) 'the constitutive element of law-making',[75] so that the people's 'consent' can make law purely out of its own strength, this means that Bartolus' discussion of that law's legal validity is in an important sense vacuous. It means that his detailed pondering of both the validity and scope of application of statutes and customs *in light of Roman law* is no more than rhetorical window-dressing to bestow an air of juristic respectability on a foregone conclusion. If there is no legal possibility that the city's say-so can be legally invalid, then there is no legal reason for its validity either. The very talk of its validity is misplaced. Validity is intrasystemic: it is relative to a normative framework or order (chapter 2.II, feature (iv)). On the proposed reading, Bartolus' entire endeavour is a methodological non-starter from the word go.

---

enforceable character to a rule of action'); on the significance of consent in the writings of medieval political thinkers (other than Bartolus), see B Tierney, *Religion, Law, and the Growth of Constitutional Thought 1150–1650* (Cambridge, Cambridge University Press, 1982) 33ff.

74 J Black, 'Constitutional ambitions, legal realities and the Florentine state' in WJ Connell and A Zorzi (eds), *Florentine Tuscany: Structures and Practices of Power* (Cambridge, Cambridge University Press, 2000) 57–8.

75 Canning, *The Political Thought of Baldus de Ubaldis*, 96.

V. OVERCOMING THE DILEMMA

But this reading is mistaken. Bartolus takes neither horn of the above dilemma. He squares the legal circle by showing the dilemma to be fallacious. His appeal to the idea of validity is not devised to generate a mere illusion of legally controlled law-making. Nor does he hold that the jurisdiction of customary law is legally unlimited.[76] No doubt a number of his arguments verge on caricature. But those are the arguments referring to the presence or absence of the Emperor's consent. Bartolus has no qualms massaging the authorities in order to get the issue of the Emperor's consent out of the way. For that is not the main issue for him. In fact it is not an issue at all. Consent *as such* is not truly an issue – whether by the Emperor or by the people.

Let us revisit his reasoning on the Venetian statute. The three main of arguments he offers in his own voice (arguments (a), (b) and (c)) concern not the Emperor's consent but the consistency of the two-witness rule

---

76 Ullmann (*Principles of Government and Politics in the Middle Ages*, 197), on whom Waldron relies (*Law and Disagreement*, 63), provides no citation in support of the proposition that '[n]o emperor, king or pope had any say in the people's own usages and customs'. Canning's (*The Political Thought of Baldus de Ubaldis*, note 14 at 96) only relevant citation is to a linguistically unhappy sentence in Bartolus' *Commentary to Digest, 1, 1, 9*, s. 4 (*quando populus habet omnem iurisdictionem potest facere statutum, non expectata superioris auctoritate* [references omitted]. *Et quod isto casu non expectetur superioris auctoritas, patet exemplo consuetudinis, quae inducitur ex tacito consensu populi, et equiparatur statuto, in qua constat quod non requiratur superioris auctoritas*). Here Bartolus seems to say that, because customs do not require authorisation by a superior, and statutes are analogous to customs, statutes do/should not require an authorisation either. But the proposition that customs do not require an authorisation must be understood in the context of the debate among commentators on whether a people can make customs *at all* or instead have transferred to the Emperor the power to make them (through his tacit consent) (on this debate, Brie, *Gewohnheitsreicht*, 151ff; on the glossators' take, 103, 113–4). Bartolus' view is that a people can make customs, but this is not yet to say that such customs are valid *even if they contradict Roman law*. The latter question is treated by Bartolus again and again as a moot point (eg *Commentary to Digest*, 1, 3, 32, s. 28; *Commentary to Code, 1, 1, 1*, ss. 21–3); as Brie (*Gewohnheitsrecht*, 119–21, 157–9) carefully shows, the question is disputed among both glossators and commentators (on Bartolus' negative answer, see ibid 158–9; and an early essay of Ullmann, in W Ullmann, *Jurisprudence in the Middle Ages* (London, Variorum Reprints, 1980) 280–1). Note also that the sentence in question appears under heading (1) of the *Commentary to Digest 1, 1, 9*, which only concerns *who* can make statutes, and is followed by heading (3), which concerns *on what matters* statutes can validly be made.

with other rules of Roman law. He draws an analogy between the rules of witnessing and the rules of probate; he flags up the special case of fathers validly making wills before two witnesses; and he points to the framework Roman provision for 'every people' to be governed by laws 'partly peculiar to itself'. Those arguments are sound. They show scholarly insight and rigour. Here we see a lawyer's zeal to keep faith with the governing legal regime, which is profusely invoked as support to each major argument he advances (and hence not of arguments (d) and (e), which are clearly residual). Bartolus pays mere lip service to the Roman Emperor. But he is unwaveringly committed to Roman *law*.

Hence his dictum that 'the [law is] valid even if the Emperor knows nothing of [it]' is not, as it might seem, a further step up from his predecessors towards deference to fact. It is the restoration of law. It captures Bartolus' decoupling of Roman *law*, as a standing set of propositions, from the Roman *Emperor*, as a human sovereign.[77] It is law that controls, and it is law that both confers power on cities and circumscribes that power. Cities may not legislate in breach of natural, international or divine law: legislation in breach of these standards, he says, is invalid (*non valeat*).[78] But legislation may not contradict Roman law either, *unless*, that is, *Roman law itself so provides.*[79] In the eyes of Bartolus, Roman law regulates the conditions

---

77 On this decoupling by Bartolus, see also Woolf, *Bartolus of Sassoferrato*, 196ff.

78 Bartolus, *Commentary to Digest, 1, 1, 9*, ss. 21–5; Woolf, *Bartolus of Sassoferrato*, 45ff; 149–5.

79 In his *Commentary to Digest, 1, 1, 9*, ss. 21–35, when explaining 'on what matters' local laws can be made, Bartolus makes it sound as though local laws could only appropriately relate to Roman law as specifications of particulars left open in the Roman corpus: he says that local laws are valid provided that (inter alia) they do not ordain what Roman law expressly forbids – having just said, in a similar vein, that human laws in general can distinguish (amplify) but not override divine law (*ius civile potest distinguere, non tollere ius divinum*: s. 22). This echoes the idea of '*determinationes*' put forward by Aquinas (*Summa Theologiae*, part I–II, question 95, article 2 (answer)), whom Bartolus is familiar with (Woolf, *Bartolus of Sassoferrato*, 17). In truth, however, in many of Bartolus' examples the inferior law does not just 'determine' (specify) but on its face *contradicts* the superior law: consider eg the Venetian two-witness rule in respect of the Roman seven-witness rule, or the latter rule itself in respect of the rule of divine law that 'in the mouth of two or three witnesses every word shall stand' (*in ore duorum vel trium stat omne verbum*: Corinthians I, 14:29; Corinthians II, 13:1; Matthew 18:16; Deutoronomy 19:15; discussed in Bartolus, *Commentary to Digest, 1, 1, 9*, s. 22). That Roman law remains a legal limit even when it is in fact not heeded is demonstrated by Bartolus' 'Treatise on Tyranny' (*Tractatus de Tyrannia*), which launches an attack on tyrannical government on strictly *legal* grounds (see Woolf, *Bartolus of Sassoferrato*, 169).

under which it may be departed from. Roman law, so to speak, consists both of framework provisions, such as the provision that every people is governed by law 'peculiar to itself', and of substantive rules, such as the rule that wills must have seven witnesses. Substantive rules amount to a sort of fallback positive regime that, as noted earlier in this chapter, may be displaced by local legislation. (And this would often be the case particularly with regimes on testamentary formalities, both local and canon.)[80] But even when it is so displaced, the Roman framework provisions remain in charge. They control every legal reasoning exercise, including the reasoning that *this* local law takes precedence over substantive Roman rules. This is why Bartolus resorts to *Roman* authorities to defend the proposition that a *Roman* rule on wills may be departed from.

In appealing to the distinction between framework rules and substantive rules of Roman law I do not mean to suggest that Roman rules come in separated camps. This is not a distinction between two groups of Roman rules but between two possible functions of Roman rules. One and the same rule may be put to either use. We must bear in mind that what we call Roman 'rules' ('provisions', 'precepts') may be anything from textbook snippets, case reports, juristic commentary or imperial responses from different periods, normally removed from their original context and unsystematically collated without transposition as normative text. Ironically, it is the miscellaneous character of Roman materials that renders them distinctly malleable, apt to be capitalised on by able hands in constructing fresh juristic landscapes. For it is a new juristic landscape that Bartolus constructs. It is *new*, because for the first time it features jurisdictions that are territorially bound but recognise no political superior. And it is *juristic*, because that jurisdiction is legally controlled and conferred.

The tools that Bartolus has at his disposal are rough, and therein lies his merit. We had seen in the previous chapter how the first official Church

80 Both the Church and local law-making elites had the policy to relax the strict Roman provisions (seven witnesses) in order to facilitate the making of wills, which would often contain dispositions of property in their favour. On the miscellaneous regulations on wills in early modern Europe, see N Jansen, 'Testamentary Formalities in Early Modern Europe' in KGC Reid, MJ de Waal and R Zimmermann (eds), *Comparative Succession Law*, vol I: Testamentary Formalities (Oxford, Oxford University Press, 2011). I thank the author for helpful clarifications on point.

codification, a century before Bartolus, placed novel emphasis on the *act* of empowerment – a superior's deliberate pronouncement on another act's legal validity; someone's say-so to the effect that someone else may validly decide in the future. Roman law, considered as an empowering regime, focally lacks this feature in Bartolus' landscape. The law that empowers cities is, in an important sense, a law without a law-maker. Bartolus could have added to his predecessors' fictions in order to salvage the idea that the Emperor has consented after all. But Bartolus refuses to go along with the dilemma that his predecessors hand him over, and the logic of imperial consent which underpins it.

For the logic of imperial consent is inherently backward-looking. The Emperor consents to – confirms – a decision *already taken* by the inferior entity. By contrast, an entity is conferred power to make law through decisions to be taken *in the future*. The logic of empowerment looks forward, not back. But as long as Roman law is regarded as an emanation of the Emperor's *person*, there is little room to explain the making of local law in terms of an empowerment. City-states have started to blossom now, 800 years after Justinian. If an Emperor's blessing is needed, and none has yet come forth, it will have to be *ex post facto*. Then *either* his confirmation is decisive, and cities do not genuinely make law, *or* the confirmation is superfluous, and the law that cities make is not genuinely in need for confirmation.

Bartolus escapes this quagmire not by replacing one kind of consent with another (*to what* is a legislative assembly 'consenting' anyway?), but by altogether replacing the logic of consent with the logic of empowerment. The latter is the logic of legal validity: of law made by someone so saying *within the framework of further law* (chapter 2.II, features (ii)–(iv)) That further law Bartolus cannot find, as in modern states, in the institutional section of a constitutional document articulating who can make which law and how. Bartolus therefore assigns this role to the Roman corpus. This is not an empowerment in that most focal sense – tied to a deliberate human act – that later centuries will exalt (chapter 9.III). But it suffices to render the cities' law-making choice ('consent') a genuine exercise of power: an act that is neither a powerless request for the superior to validate, nor a legal genesis out of whole cloth.

Bartolus' 'juristic masterstroke', says Canning, lies in attributing to the city, within its territory, the same powers of jurisdiction that the Emperor wields over the Empire as a whole.[81] But note that the stroke is masterful precisely because it is *juristic* – controlled by law. This reveals a constitutionalist mindset that is sensitive to the Rule of Law (chapter 9.III). It also foreshadows the move that Hart will famously make as against Austin's insistence that there is a person, not a rule, at the foundations of a legal order.[82] Bartolus writes two centuries after Gratian. Canon lawyers are the first to put the fruits of Roman legal study at the service of constructing a new legal system. The transformation in the secular domain takes longer but is all the more pervasive. Canon lawyers need a universal law for a universal organisation. Secular lawyers have a received universal law but territorially bound rulers. Provisions premised on the one-empire model are not fit for purpose, without more. Canon law contemplates jurisdictional limits based on institutional hierarchy and an overriding divine or natural law. Secular practice calls for a novel kind of jurisdictional limit, a limit marked by geographic boundaries. The word 'territory', says Bartolus, is derived from 'terrify'.[83] The remark is inaccurate but suggestive. Cities have a distinct territory when they can effectively use force to vindicate it. That is a fact. Bartolus' reasoning, like all sound legal reasoning, takes account of the empirical world. In so doing he remains both true to fact and true to law.

A Copernican turn is coming about at this time in our legal culture, perhaps comparable to that triggered by the classical Roman jurist (chapter 3). Bartolus, like the Roman jurist, seeks to overcome the inadequacies of the received body of law by exploiting the resources available in it. Those resources are not positive law pure and simple. Law and legal science are closely intertwined in Bartolus' time, as they are in the Roman era. For Bartolus, Roman law is not a set of provisions that may in turn be the object of a legal science or doctrinal study conducted as a separate exercise. Roman law very much *is* the science of law, and its reach extends beyond the letter of the original Justinian corpus to include embedded glosses and commentary, written and oral, old and new.[84] Roman law is a framework

---

81 Canning, *The Political Thought of Baldus de Ubaldis*, 96, see also Bellomo, *The Common Legal Past of Europe*, 191–2, 158.

82 HLA Hart, *The Concept of Law*, 2nd edn (Oxford, Clarendon Press, 1994) chapter 4.

83 Bartolus, *Commentary to Code, 1, 1, 1*, s. 46, citing Justinian, *Digest*, 50, 16, 239, 8.

84 Woolf, *Bartolus of Sassoferrato*, 13–4. On the development of the relationship between law and legal science from medieval to modern times, see N Jansen, *Rechtswissenschaft und Rechtssystem: Sieben Thesen nur Positivierung des Rechts und zur Differenzierung von Recht und Rechtswissenschaft*, Würzburger Vorträge zur Rechtsphilosophie, Rechtstheorie und Rechtssoziologie, vol 56 (Baden-Baden, Nomos Verlag, 2018), especially thesis 3 (21–32).

law also because it is a science. And because it is a science, as Bartolus sees it, it need not be gapless, and may well be amenable to improvement, just as scientific advances build upon the errors of their predecessors. Bartolus and his followers are less deferential to the Roman sources than glossators had been. But that does not reflect a concern to 'evolve a law practically acceptable *rather than* scientifically correct'.[85] It is the upshot of the inevitable need to select from among legal sources, in the name and for the sake of legal science.

It is that science that is taught at the new law schools, and that students from all over Europe are passionate to absorb. Roman law teaches terms, classifications, techniques of reasoning, conceptual maps. It teaches the grammar of law that local regimes will trade on.[86] Any notary giving legal clothing to a client's wishes needs to master the categories and labels that come with Roman law. A deed awarding a servitude (easement) acquires its legal meaning only in conjunction with Roman law – the law that defines the nature of servitudes, and the legal science that recognises that rights can be validly awarded through a distinct technique. Even glossators, therefore, had a practical reason to want to distil Roman law. Transformed social relations in increasingly urban environments assign a new place to law, and that place is focally filled not *by* the grammar of Roman law but *through* it, *by means of* it, in the way that a shared linguistic grammar enables communication of the most miscellaneous content. Latin at that time operates throughout Europe as the common language (*lingua franca*), from which derive the 'vulgar tongues' peculiar to each territory (Italian, Spanish, French, Catalan, etc). So, too, the grammar of Roman law, and with it the grammar of legal validity, is looked to as making up a common law (*ius commune*) in European lands.[87] It is a law that is common because capable of being shared by individuals in different predicaments, points of time, locations, and eventually national environments.

---

85 Woolf, *Bartolus of Sassoferrato*, 387 (my emphasis).

86 See further Bellomo, *The Common Legal Past of Europe*, 152ff; Padoa-Schioppa, *A History of Law in Europe*, 205. On how Roman law (more generally, the *ius commune*) bears on the interpretation of local law, see ibid 205–7.

87 On the unifying role of Latin, Christianity and legal science, see Bellomo, *The Common Legal Past of Europe*, 178–9. On the complex idea of the *ius commune*, see N Jansen, '*Ius commune* (Gemeines Recht)' in J Basedow, KJ Hopt and R Zimmermann (eds), *Handwörterbuch des Europäischen Privatrechts* (Tübingen, Mohr Siebeck, 2009). On how and why medieval legal scholars develop a self-contained legal grammar that, in being narrowly focused on Roman sources, is apt to be widely shared, see N Jansen, *Rechtswissenschaft und Rechtssystem*, thesis 2 (14–20).

In the *ius commune*'s method lies the key for its success. To the extent that Roman law stands as a body of rules detached from an imperial law-maker, emerging sovereign states see no inconsistency in adopting this body of rules while challenging the fading ambitions of a world ruler. Decoupling Roman *law* from the Roman *Emperor* is a prerequisite for Roman law to make its way into our modern legal orders.[88] Legal validity takes the West from a 'world state' to a world of states.

---

88 In this spirit, Woolf, *Bartolus of Sassoferrato*, 44.

CHAPTER 8

SUAREZ (EARLY 17TH)

Inherent Legal Power

I. THE SCHOOL OF NATURAL LAW

By the sixteenth century, the *ius commune* has to varying degrees impregnated, even blended with, the positive law of European political communities.[1] These communities increasingly take the shape of nation states in a world whose cultural and territorial confines are understood to reach well beyond the 'old continent'. Legal scholarship diversifies its lines of enquiry, over and above doctrinal engagement with the immediate

---

1 On the manifold kinds of 'Reception' process of Roman law, see eg T Duve, 'Von der Europäischen Rechtsgeschichte zu einer Rechtsgeschichte Europas in globalhistorischer Perspektive' (2012) 20 *Rechtsgeschichte* 18, especially 31ff; MT Fögen and G Teubner, 'Rechtstransfer' (2005) 7 *Rechtsgeschichte* 38.

concerns of lawyerly practice. Self-consciously historical and philosophical studies add to the growing body of legal thought that dares to take on a canvas broader than the writer's own jurisdiction.

The School of Natural Law aims to explain how positive law can and does embody true rational principles – principles of right reason, 'natural law'. In so arguing, the School builds on the *ius commune*, which furnishes positive law's central conceptual apparatus. But the School's work profoundly influences the *ius commune* in turn. It lays the foundations for the later codification movement (chapter 9.II). That is so not least because systematicity ranks high in the agenda of Natural Law theorists, as it did in the agenda of glossators and early canon lawyers, albeit on different grounds. Then it was the inaugural retrieval of a long buried treasure, and its service in a complex legal system's founding hour. It is now, amongst other things, a general devising of the forms of social arrangement best suited to address important human needs in an ever more interdependent and technically sophisticated world.

Francisco de Suarez is a Granada-born scholar in the Natural Law tradition. He writes a voluminous work titled *Tractatus de Legibus ac Deo Legislatore* (Treatise on Laws and God as Legislator), which appears in 1612. The work's discussion of legal validity in the context of transactions is of pioneering depth and precision. Many insights that contemporary scholars attribute to Hart find in Suarez an early ground-breaking, and in some ways more subtle, articulation. As opposed to the authors of the landmark texts we have surveyed so far, Suarez writes as a legal theorist. His engagement with legal validity therefore reaches a level of reflexivity not evidenced in the earlier texts. Suarez writes *about* the laws that set out rules *about* legal validity. His treatment of the validity of transactions constitutes a critical link between the incipiently systematic medieval thought and the entrenched deployment of validity in the age of codification.

But even Suarez's comparatively unfocussed treatment of the validity of enactments is telling. For it goes to explain why it took yet another couple of centuries for legal thought to openly embrace the understanding, latent in Bartolus, that law-making is itself a creature of law. The latter half of the title of Suarez's work harbours a clue.

This chapter separately traces Suarez's discussions of transactions and law-making, before turning to the troubling tension between the two.

We may note at the outset that Suarez's text, as might be expected, makes a profuse use of the full range of 'validity' terms we have hitherto identified, including the adjective '*validum*' and the adverb '*valide*'. *In*validity is predominantly expressed through the terms '*irritum*' (and '*irritare*'), '*nullum*' and '*non valet*'. Suarez uses the noun '*valor*' (value) in preference to '*validitas*', albeit in just that sense.

II. VALIDITY OF TRANSACTIONS

The validity of transactions occupies extensive argument in the first, second and fifth Books of Suarez's ten-book treatise. These Books deal respectively with (a) laws in general, (b) eternal law, natural law and *ius gentium*, and (c) human laws. As we will see, although Suarez portrays the validity of transactions as a subject matter germane to *human* laws (civil and canon), he also regards it as having some implications in contemplation of natural law. The human laws that concern the legal validity of transactions he dubs '*leges irritantes*' – literally, invalidating laws. Like Bartolus, therefore, Suarez approaches the subject matter of the validity of transactions from the point of view of the *laws* regulating it. This is in line with his work's framing concern (*De Legibus*). Indeed, he first broaches the topic of the validity of transactions, towards the end of Book One, in reflecting on the different kinds of effects that laws may have (*effectus legis*).[2] Recall that in the Digest these effects are said to be fourfold: to command, to prohibit, to permit and to punish (*imperare*, *vetare*, *permittere*, *punire*).[3] This is Modestinus' classical division of the functions of law. Suarez only nominally seeks to preserve the purportedly exhaustive character of the Roman list.[4] For, in every significant respect, his *leges irritantes* make up a robustly distinct category of laws, not reducible in their function or logic to those four kinds.

---

2 F de Suarez, *Tractatus De Legibus ac Deo Legislatore (De Legibus)*, beginning at [book] 1, [chapter] 15, [section] 1. (I follow the section subdivision in the Latin/Spanish edition F Suarez, *Tratado de las Leyes y de Dios Legislador* (Madrid, Instituto de Estudios Políticos, 1967), which claims to be based on the work's *editio princeps*.).

3 Justinian, *Digest*, 1, 3, 7 (Modestinus) (see also chapter 5.II and chapter 7.II of this book).

4 Suarez, *De Legibus*, 1, 17, 8–10 (on how *leges irritantes* belong to the categories of prohibition and precept, including the idea of a prohibiting *lex irritante* as involving, in a sense, a 'double prohibition').

Suarez brings out the distinctness of *leges irritantes* primarily by contrasting invalidity to prohibition. He insists that they are very different effects (*prohibire actum, et irritare illum, sunt effectus valde diversi*),[5] and that they cut across one another. Of course an act may be both prohibited and invalid,[6] but it may also be prohibited and valid, or invalid but not prohibited. To these last two possibilities he devotes illuminating passages.

The idea that acts may be *prohibited but valid* was already touched on in the Gloss to Gratian's *Decretum*, for example when it noted that certain acts '*tenet*' (hold) despite being '*contra legem*' (against a law/legal prohibition) (chapter 5.III). The idea also underlay the *Decretals*' articulation of, inter alia, impedient (prohibiting) and diriment (invalidating) marriage impediments (chapter 6.II). But in Suarez it is the object of an extensive theoretical defence, not least in the course of a critical engagement with the Roman *lex non dubium*, that imperial law according to which every legal prohibition should be understood to entail invalidation unless otherwise specified (chapter 3.I–II). In opposition to this, Suarez argues that invalidation must not be presumed.[7] He approvingly invokes the maxim that 'many prohibited things are nevertheless valid if done' (*multa fieri prohibentur, quae tamen facta tenant*).[8] The law-giver may favour an act in terms of its validity and effect, despite not favouring it in terms of its malice (*malitiae*). So the act may be valid even though it is wrong to perform it (*ideo licet actus male fiar, validus est*).[9] This can be true, for instance, of sales for more than the item's just price, of sinfully celebrated

5 ibid 5, 25, 22; also 1, 17, 8 (*irritatio dicit specialem effectum a prohibitione distinctum*). As he sometimes succinctly puts it, 'to invalidate is not to order but to do' (*irritare non est precipere, sed facere*, 2, 12, 2; also 5, 20, 14; 5, 25, 22).

6 See ibid 2, 12, 4–5 on some general rules about when an act prohibited by natural law is also invalid.

7 ibid, especially at 5, 25–8. Grotius, in his treatise *De Iure Belli ac Pacis Libri Tres. In quibus ius naturae & Gentium: item iuris publici praecipua explicantur* (Paris, Nicolas Buon, 1625), makes an analogous, if less extensive, case against a general presumption of invalidity arising from prohibition. Focusing on unlawful marriages, he likewise insists on the difference between prohibiting and voiding (*irritare*) (see eg ibid book 2, chapter 5, section 16). He tries to reconcile this position with the *lex non dubium*, arguing that the transactions concerned are not invalid in virtue of the legal prohibition alone, but in virtue of the *lex non dubium* itself – a reading hard to square with the latter's own claim that it states the rule (only) for the avoidance of doubt. Grotius also somewhat inaccurately likens such legal prohibitions to *leges imperfectae* in Ulpian's sense (see chapter 3.I of this book).

8 Suarez, *De Legibus*, 5, 25, 3.

9 ibid 5, 25, 25.

consecrations, of marriages in breach of prohibiting but not invalidating impediments, or of judgments wrongly given subject to condition.[10]

But perhaps the most significant move of Suarez, in relation to his predecessors, is his candid contemplation of the converse predicament: that of acts *invalid but not prohibited*. He has a somewhat roundabout way of framing the question. He says that *leges irritantes*, invalidating laws, may invalidate an act directly or indirectly.[11] They invalidate it *indirectly* when they determine a *form* as being essential for the act's validity. They invalidate it *directly* when they invalidate the act hand in hand with *prohibiting* it. Examples of the former include rules on the procedure for valid marriages and on the number of witnesses for valid wills – these are rules of the kind that served as Bartolus' focus when he discussed the validity of transactions (chapter 7.II). Examples of the latter rules mentioned by Suarez include rules on serious contractual fraud and on breach of diriment marriage impediments (such as consanguinity, to a defined degree) – these are rules of the kind that served as the canonists' focus. In jointly contemplating and categorising these two sets of rules, Suarez comes close to charting a distinction amongst *grounds* of invalidity. And that distinction is a crucial step in making explicit what was only implicit in those earlier works. Namely: there are grounds of invalidity other than prohibition, because it takes certain positive (eg formal, procedural) requirements for an act to be valid in the first place, which requirements are themselves determined by law (chapter 2.II, feature (iii)).[12]

Suarez comes closest to portraying this positive, validating role of law when he explains why *leges irritantes* that determine the form of acts (and so 'invalidate indirectly') do not 'prohibit in conscience'.[13] Seeing as they prescribe a form, he says, they are affirmative precepts, and as such they are not absolute but conditional. They only order that (say) *if* a certain

10 In relation to this last example, Suarez (*De Legibus*, 5, 25, 13) points to the very passage in the *Decretum*'s Gloss that we had flagged up before (Gloss to '*dissolui*' at Gratian, *Decretum*, D. 10, c. 10).

11 Suarez, *De Legibus*, 1, 17, 9–10; 5, 19, 4.

12 Suarez briefly puts it in similar terms at the start of his discussion of *leges irritantes*: '*aliquae conditiones sunt iure humano requisitae, sine quibus contractus non est validus ex vi eiusdem iuris humani*' (*De Legibus*, 5, 19, 1 pr).

13 Suarez, *De Legibus*, 5, 20. Compare Bartolus' similar, but unexplained, distinction between criminal prohibitions and laws 'prohibitive otherwise than criminally' (chapter 8.II above).

sale is made, it is to be made in certain *way*.[14] Unless it is a sacrilege or otherwise wrongful to ignore that form in particular, the law in question is 'purely invalidating'.[15] Unlike a legal prohibition, it does not oblige in conscience. It is not a sin to fail to make a solemn will.[16] The will's invalidity is not a punishment; instead, the solemnity is provided 'so that justice is more *securely* served'.[17] The main reason why *leges irritantes* ought to be published, therefore, is that 'it is necessary that people know how they can and should perform their actions for them to be valid'.[18]

This is not far from the Hartian idea that laws thus provide facilities for people to realise their wishes, rather than prescribing what they must or must not do.[19] Suarez's discussion of *leges irritantes* also matches in other regards what contemporary legal theory casts as power-conferring rules, which broadly correspond to the understanding of the technique of validity canvassed in chapter 2. Thus Suarez clearly gestures towards the idea of a change in normative position as being the consequence of valid acting. He says, for example, that an act's being null entails that it confers no right (*actus est nullus; ergo nullum confert ius*),[20] and that an act that is 'annulled in conscience' (an idea to which I soon return) does not give rise to the relevant obligations or permissions.[21] Although Suarez does not generalise about the things amenable to being invalidated, other than by speaking generically of 'contracts' or 'acts',[22] the breadth of his examples

---

14 ibid 5, 20, 2 (*non enim praecipiunt alienationem fieri, v.g. sed ut si fiat, tali modo fiat*).

15 ibid 5, 20, 5–7.

16 ibid 5, 20, 7; 5, 19, 5.

17 ibid 3, 35, 25 (my emphasis) (*ut* securius *servetur iustitia*). In general, invalidity can coexist with prohibition precisely because it is not (normally) a penalty in itself (5, 19; 1, 17, 8; 3, 35, 24–5; 5, 25, 6).

18 Suarez, *De Legibus*, 5, 33, 1 (*quia necessarium est ut homines sciant, quomodo possint, ac debeant actiones suas facere, ut valide sint*). For helpful discussion of this and related passages in likening Suarezian *leges irritantes* to 'power-conferring rules', with an emphasis on the broad distinction between the *vis directiva* and *vis coactiva* of law (1, 17, 4; 3, 35, 24; 5, 19, 5), see J Delgado Echeverría, 'Las leges irritantes en De Legibus de Francisco Suárez como normas de competencia' (2006) 29 *DOXA Cuadernos de Filosofía del Derecho* 405.

19 HLA Hart, *The Concept of Law*, 2nd edn (Oxford, Clarendon Press, 1994) 27 et passim.

20 Suarez, *De Legibus*, 5, 10, 14.

21 ibid 5, 32, 6–7.

22 The first reference is to 'contracts, wills, etc.' (Suarez, *De Legibus*, 1, 17, 1); at 2, 12 it is 'acts'; at 5, 19, 1 it is initially 'contracts' in a broad sense that includes wills and marriages; at 5, 31, 1 it is first 'acts', then 'acts or contracts'.

leaves no doubt that he focally has in mind what we now call transactions. Central to the performance of these acts, he says, is the individual will.[23]

One might therefore wonder why Suarez gives these laws a negative name after all – why, in other words, they are *invalidating* (*irritantes*) rather than validating or enabling rules. Note that this is not quite the same puzzle as we faced concerning Bartolus' classification of the relevant laws. There we wondered why Bartolus would say of certain laws that set validity criteria that they are 'prohibitive' (invalidating) *as opposed to* 'permissive' (validating), and vice versa (chapter 7.II). The answer to this question, as we saw, is that Bartolus takes as his benchmark the rules of Roman law, which he regards as a positive framework regime. Relative to the rules of Roman law, local statutes either increase or decrease the requirements of legal validity. But for Suarez, it seems, *all* positive rules that deal with validity criteria are invalidating.

The reason for this is that Suarez uses an altogether different kind of benchmark. That benchmark is natural law. His explanation of the label '*irritantes*' discloses the very peculiar relationship there is, for him, between the validity of transactions and the idea of power – a relationship very different from the one nominally envisaged by Hart. According to Suarez,

> Human will has by natural law the power [*potestas*] to enter contracts, make gifts and similar things, so long as a superior does not remove or impede this ability ...[24]

Hence:

> In order for an act to be valid, it is not necessary, strictly speaking, that it is supported or positively assisted by the superior's will or by human law; it is enough that the latter do not oppose the act by invalidating it.[25]

---

23 Suarez, *De Legibus*, 5, 19, 4; 2, 12, 4. He expressly associates power and will ('without power and without will no valid act can be made': 2, 12, 4).

24 ibid 5, 25, 25 (*voluntas humana ex iure naturae habet hanc potestatem contrahendi, donandi, et alia similia faciendi, quamdiu per superiorem eius facultas non est ablata, vel impedita*).

25 ibid 5, 25, 25 (*Quia ut actus valeat, non est necessarium, per se loquendo, ut superioris voluntas vel humanum ius iuvet, vel assistant illi positive, sed satis est, quod non resistat irritando*).

The role of *leges irritantes* is thus to remove or curb a power the existence of which they presuppose.[26] The power in question is a pre-legal, 'moral power' (*potestas moralis*), which is the 'first foundation' and the 'root' of the act's validity.[27] *Leges irritantes* may take away such natural or moral power compatibly with natural law because, Suarez explains, experience shows that this is often necessary in order to prevent fraud and other kinds of inconvenience (*ad vitandas fraudes et alia incommoda*).[28] A man may be deprived of his power to make contracts 'just as he may be deprived of his freedom'.[29] To be clear: what Suarez is saying applies even to 'purely invalidating' laws, that is, to laws that merely set procedural or formal requirements for an act to be valid. Indeed, Suarez draws on the idea of removing (*privare, tollere*) power in order to further sharpen the *distinction* between invalidation and prohibition. Invalidation, unlike (mere) prohibition, removes the 'absolute power' to perform the act (*absolutam potestatem faciendi actum*).[30] A law that determines the formalities for making a will, on this view, removes the 'absolute power' to make the will in any other way. In this sense it curbs or impedes an ability that would otherwise be inherent in persons by virtue of natural law.

This is doubtless a coherent view about the moral justification of *leges irritantes*, of positive laws that regulate validity. On this view, they are primarily called for as a constraint on human autonomy, as a necessary evil, rather than as a facilitating amenity. Their point is to reduce rather than amplify the scope of human action. Legal validity places a justified, morally needed limit on what persons may do by way of forging relationships and commitments.

Suarez, however, goes on to qualify this view about the relationship between *leges irritantes* and inherent power in two significant ways at an unexpected juncture. The second qualification even smacks of contradiction.

The context in which these qualifications occur is Suarez's discussion of the question whether invalidation should be presumed in the case of laws that

---

26 ibid 5, 31, 15 (*lex supponit potestatem ad actum*).

27 ibid 5, 31, 11 (*quia cum potestas sit primum fundamentum valoris actus, qui negat potestatem, tollit radicem valoris*); 2, 12, 4; 5, 31, 15.

28 ibid 5, 19, 1.

29 ibid 5, 19, 1.

30 ibid 1, 17, 8 (*Nam prohibitio, ut sic, non tollit absolutam potestatem faciendi actum, sed facit, ne liceat; at irritatio privat potestate faciendi valide actum; est ergo effectus distinctus*).

determine form or procedure. We already noted his negative answer to this question in respect of laws that prohibit an act: *pace* the *lex non dubium*, says Suarez, invalidation should not be presumed. But should form and procedure always be understood as prescribed *on pain of invalidity*? Should, in other words, all rules that somehow regulate form or procedure be automatically deemed to be *leges irritantes*?

Suarez's immediate answer is negative again: invalidation is 'odious',[31] 'somehow it removes a natural right [*naturale ius*]',[32] and must therefore be narrowly construed. But – here comes the first qualification – not in respect of all kinds of act. This is the one time Suarez distinguishes valid decisions by public officials from valid acts of 'private property' (*private dominii*), that is, exercises of private power.[33] By acts by public officials he means acts 'such as a judgment, an election, … and all public administration or administration done with a public authority'.[34] These are relatively particular resolutions, rather than acts of general law-making. Suarez deems those particular resolutions of legal officials to be subject to *leges irritantes*. This means that, like the earlier writers we studied, Suarez regards such official resolutions as being relevantly similar to private transactions, in that both those resolutions and private transactions are amenable to being valid or invalid. But there is a difference between public and private acts when it comes to the question whether invalidity should be presumed for defect of procedure or form. In respect of public acts, he says, invalidity should be presumed. The reason: acts of public officials 'depend on a power conferred by the prince, by the state or by public authority',[35]

---

31 *Leges irritantes* are one main kind of 'odious' laws, alongside penal laws and tax laws (Suarez, *De Legibus*, 5, 2, 15).

32 Suarez, *De Legibus*, 5, 25, 24 (*quodammodo aufert quodam naturale ius*). '*Ius*', as here deployed, does not match any of the uses of the term Suarez charts at the start of his treatise (1, 2). What he there calls the 'true, strict and proper meaning' of '*ius*', namely 'a kind of moral power [*facultas*] which every man has, either over his own property or with respect to that which is due to him' (1, 2, 5), is not the ability to change legal relations but rather a kind of legal relation thereby changed, corresponding to the modern idea of 'a right' (hence his examples: an owner's right over the owned thing, worker's right to a salary); this matches Savigny's idea of '*ein Recht*' (chapter 9.I below). On Suarez's understanding of '*ius*', see J Finnis, *Natural Law and Natural Rights*, 2nd edn (Oxford, Oxford University Press, 2011) 206–7.

33 Suarez, *De Legibus*, 5, 31, 15; also called '*actus propriae auctoritatis et dominii*' (5, 31, 14). The contrast is later framed in terms of acts (and laws) that belong to the public administration, and those primarily concerned with the good of individuals (5, 32, 7).

34 ibid 5, 31, 14.

35 ibid 5, 32, 15 (*pendeat ex potestate concessa a principe, vel republica, vel ab auctoritate iuris*); the power is also referred to as '*potestate concessa a lege vel republica*' (ibid).

so that *the entity that imposes form is the very entity that confers the power in the first place.*[36] That entity is the law (or the prince). Hence, if the official does not follow the form prescribed by law, he is unable to exercise the power, for the source of this power is the prescribing law itself.

This qualification entails that Suarez's earlier claims about the inherent 'moral power' to act validly hold only in respect of private transactions, not official acts. *Leges irritantes* can freshly *confer* power after all: namely, when they govern acts of legal officials. The second qualification, in turn, softens the extent to which *leges irritantes* truly *remove* that 'moral power' when they invalidate private transactions. Even when a law expressly prescribes a form on pain of invalidity, and so invalidates a non-compliant transaction, the law's invalidating import may not reach as far as to efface the 'natural validity' of the private act.[37] For – and this is critical – the law annuls an act legally, and thus externally (*in foro exteriori*). It need not annul the act absolutely or 'in conscience' (*in conscientia*). Suarez actually gives the example of a will that has not been executed following the relevant solemnities. That will, he says, cannot serve as evidence in trial or ground a legal claim – in this sense, the law annuls the act legally or externally. But whoever is named heir under it may justifiably keep the inheritance until, if ever, he is legally challenged – in this sense, the act does not annul the act absolutely or 'in conscience'. The law annuls the instrument of the will (*testamentum*) but not the will (*voluntatem*) of the deceased.

It follows that failing to make a solemn will not only is not sinful, on Suarez's account, but it may not even curb the act's 'natural validity'. *Leges irritantes* may annul (*irritare*) an act and yet, it seems, not remove the 'absolute power' to perform it – the very feature he had presented as the mark of *leges irritantes.*

III. VALIDITY OF ENACTMENTS

Let us briefly set aside this problem in order to explore Suarez's discussion in the domain of law-making. Here the idea of *leges irritantes* is wholly absent. *Leges irritantes* are a species of laws made, not (also) laws that

36 ibid 5, 31, 14.

37 ibid 5, 32, 6–7 (*leges non irritare obligationem internam, nec impedire naturalem valorem actus*).

regulate the way to make laws. In fact Suarez only sometimes applies the idea of validity to laws and law-making acts. Laws and transactions stand, in Suarez's thought, in a very different order, almost as the divine stands to the human. It is not that Suarez denies or downplays the fact that human laws are positive, decided on and promulgated by humans. He has a robust grasp, as we will see in a moment, of the human acts involved in making law. It is rather that he envisages the power to make laws as, in a very important sense, *conferred on humans by God*, and conferred precisely with the restriction that only just laws can be made in its exercise.[38] One upshot of this is that, as Suarez stresses again and again, an unjust law is not a law (*lex iniusta non est lex*):[39] an unjust provision cannot be valid (*non potest esse valida*), and true human law cannot validly prescribe (*non potest valide praecipere*) other than just and honest things.[40] Another related upshot is that all laws 'obligate in conscience' once duly promulgated and accessible to addressees.[41] Law-makers legislate as ministers of God.[42]

In this regard, therefore, Suarez's account of the validity of enactments is further away from our modern understanding than Bartolus' account was. Suarez makes an unpalatable association of the validity of enactments and their moral binding force, whereas Bartolus incipiently considers Roman law as a strictly *legal* limit on law-making. In another regard, however, it is Suarez's thought that is closer to modern constitutionalist tenets, as I go on to show. Whereas Bartolus' account has little logical space for deliberate *acts* of official empowerment, in Suarez we find an avant-garde account of both the idea of delegation of power, and of its exercise through a manifestation of will.

Take the latter point first. Suarez is very clear that this is how law-making power is exercised.[43] The ruler's will 'is no more than the will to manifest to the subject the will to obligate him'.[44] It is therefore a will to

38 ibid 1, 9, 18.

39 In reference to Aquinas, *Summa Theologiae*, part I–II, question 96, article 4 (answer); question 95, article 2 (answer).

40 Suarez, *De Legibus*, 1, 9, 4; also eg 1, 1, 6; 6, 25, 2; 3, 19, 11; 3, 22, 1. Official resolutions concerning dispensation or abrogation of laws, by contrast, may be both unjust and valid (6, 10ff).

41 ibid 3, 17; 3, 21; 3, 22.

42 ibid 3, 21, 6.

43 ibid 1, 4, 4 (*manifestante voluntatem superioris*); 3, 15, 1–2; passim.

44 ibid 3, 20, 5.

obligate by means of that manifestation.[45] Suarez likens this will to the 'soul' of the law, and speaks of the 'external sign or matter' wherein the law is manifested as the law's 'body'.[46] By this Suarez is not referring to the law's public promulgation, but to the legislator's casting his thoughts into language (chapter 2.II, feature (ii)). As he carefully explains, the law's 'bodily' manifestation must be of a kind suited to human perception and understanding, as written words characteristically are[47] – though any verbal form will do, he adds, as long as the words 'sufficiently manifest that the sovereign's intention is to give a stable [and] general precept'.[48] Suarez even appreciates that the 'essence' of that 'bodily' mark is its *meaning* (*significatio*).[49]

Such an act of law-making is an exercise of *power* on Suarez's account. The power in question is 'jurisdictional', he says, as opposed to being sheer power as influence.[50] The idea of jurisdictional power, reminiscent of Bartolus, denotes power to legislate and thus to bind others. Ultimately this power is God's, we are told, because only God can justly punish and obligate in conscience.[51] But God bestows this power on complete ('perfect') human communities (which Suarez assumes to be territorially bound). Communities need power to govern themselves (*regime sui ipsius*)[52] and they, in turn, transfer this power to specific sovereign individuals such as emperors or kings.[53] This is why the latter can justly and validly give laws (*valide ... condere potest*) by observing the other conditions for law-giving specified by the relevant civil law[54] – conditions that natural law underdetermines but that have to be settled so subjects can know when a law 'has been sufficiently established'.[55] (Only in this tenuous sense is there a *legal* limit on law-making.)

---

45 He phrases it elliptically: 'the will to obligate, if effective, includes the will to manifest oneself and make oneself known externally to the subject, for without this manifestation there can be no obligation' (Suarez, *De Legibus*, 3, 20, 6). He also says that obligation is the object of the manifested will because the legislator does not have the power to bring about actual compliance, but only to obligate (1, 4, 6–8).

46 Suarez, *De Legibus*, 3, 15, 1; 1, 4, 4.

47 ibid 1, 4, 5; 3, 15, 6.

48 ibid 3, 15, 7. The legislator's intention is to be presumed from the words (3, 20, 7).

49 ibid 3, 15, 2.

50 ibid 1, 8, 4ff.

51 ibid 3, 3, 1–3.

52 ibid 3, 1–3.

53 ibid 3, 4, 8; 3, 4, 11.

54 ibid 3, 1, 6.

55 ibid 3, 16, 5.

Sovereign individuals who thus hold jurisdictional power can, on their part, *delegate* it on other individuals or institutions, such as judges or the Senate.[56] To delegate power, according to Suarez, is to entrust someone with the publication of a provision so that he can give it authority through his own will.[57] Delegation of power is a more genuinely legal, intrasystemic phenomenon than the (necessarily preceding) conferral of power by God on the community, and by the community on the sovereign. Indeed, delegated power (*potestas delegata*), says Suarez, cannot be delegated further.[58] Although he does not canvass the relations amongst the different organs of what we would today call the state's public administration, his account commits him to regarding all such organs as holders of jurisdictional power, at least by delegation. Consistently with this, he notes that jurisdictional power comes in degrees: judges have jurisdiction but they cannot legislate, because making law calls for 'superior and principal' jurisdictional power.[59]

IV. A TROUBLING CONTACT POINT

It is time to pull together the threads of Suarez's discussion, and we should do so by considering the topic of particular official decisions. Particular official decisions, such as judgments or administrative decrees, have a place both in Suarez's account of law-making and in his account of transactions. These decisions are the silenced and troubling contact point between the two accounts. It is silenced because Suarez never flags up this area of convergence. It is troubling because the accounts are not as compatible as they would need to be in order to be able to converge. *On the one hand*, Suarez treats official decisions as acts subject to *leges irritantes*. But *leges irritantes*, he has told us, determine validity quite independently of prohibition. Therefore, acts subject to these laws may be prohibited but valid. And since prohibitions track wrongful behaviour, and therefore

56 The principal sovereign may also confer jurisdictional power to 'cities or inferior sovereigns' (Suarez, *De Legibus*, 3, 4, 11; 1, 8, 9); technically this is not a mere 'delegation' but is closer to the kind of transferral of power that occurs between the community and the principal sovereign. Such transferral involves giving and receiving power 'as ordinary', not 'as delegated': 3, 4, 9. Suarez even characterises this kind of transferral as 'almost an alienation' (*quasi alienatio*: 3, 4, 11).

57 Suarez, *De Legibus*, 3, 4, 10.

58 ibid 3, 4, 12.

59 ibid 1, 8, 8.

bind in conscience, the relevant acts may be wrongful but valid. An unjust transaction is still a transaction. An unjust judgment – on this logic – is still a judgment. But, *on the other hand*, Suarez explains that the powers of public officials partake in the ultimately divinely founded jurisdictional power, from which no unjust precept can validly issue (*non potest esse valida*). An unjust law is not a law. An unjust judgment – on this logic – is not either.

It might be thought that this conundrum simply comes down to an unhappily narrow use of 'validity' in respect of law-making. Suarez's only fault, it might be said, is not to have reserved the term 'validity' to capture the sense in which even unjust laws exist and are treated as laws in strictly legal argument, a sense he obscures by focusing on the moral binding force of laws rather than on the way their production is legally regulated. But this impasse has a curious analogue at the opposite end of the legal spectrum, namely in respect of the power to make private transactions. This power he portrays as being inherent in individuals. This means that this power *is not conferred by positive law* either. And here as well, Suarez's holding on to this premise breeds inconsistency. That is the problem we left hanging at the end of section II of this chapter. The 'moral power' of individuals is sometimes left intact by the laws whose effect is to remove it. In the private realm, that is. For the inconsistency does not arise in the realm of official acts, which are exercises of a power bestowed by the very laws that regulate it. It is a power that, as per the account of law-making, is conferred through the intrasystemic delegating acts of other officials.

It follows that only in the thinly charted intermediate domain of particular official decisions, only in this unspoken hinge between two worlds apparently divided by a metaphysical gulf, is power *legally* conferred in Suarez's account. And only in respect of this domain is the account free from the infelicities we have canvassed.

Suppose, then, that Suarez generalised this understanding of legal power *across* all legal domains. What would the implications be for Suarez's understanding of law-making and private transactions? In respect of law-making, this would entail embracing the distinct relevance of the positive legal framework within which even a sovereign's manifestation of will (a mere say-so) acquires its meaning and import as a source of *legal* propositions (chapter 2.II, feature (iv)). This focus, in turn, would enable Suarez to explain, as he neglects to do, why justice requires that positive laws be recognisable *as laws* quite independently of their moral merit – why, in short, it is morally necessary that the validity of laws does *not* primarily turn on moral considerations.[60]

A sustained focus on legally conferred power would also expunge the inconsistency in respect of private transactions. Recall his claim that in significant cases, such as a formally deficient will, the invalidating effect of *leges irritantes* is circumscribed to the field of external action (*in foro exteriori*). By this Suarez means no more and no less than the transaction's recognition and enforcement as a matter of law. He has in mind the status of the transaction as that status is given credence in adjudicating on a legal claim, for example a legal challenge by the intestate heirs. Elsewhere, in fact, he draws a nuanced picture of the procedural implications of a transaction being (judicially) voidable rather than void ab initio.[61] It is this *legal* recognition or currency of which invalidation deprives an act in all cases (regardless of any extant 'natural validity' of the act). But this is an effect *that only laws could have bestowed on the act in the first place*. In this respect it is no longer true that '[i]n order for an act to be valid, it is not necessary … that it is … positively assisted by … human law'.[62] The reason for giving the laws a negative name also very much disappears. In an important sense, the private power *which is liable to be removed* (or withheld) is no less legally *conferred* than the power of officials in the public administration.

We must conclude that, underlying Suarez's apparently negative conception of *leges irritantes* as curbing a natural power inherent in individuals, there are solid, if scattered, elements of a rival, positive understanding of these laws as fundamentally *enabling*, as regulating and channelling the exercise of a power that in an important sense only these laws can confer. It is the power to make and unmake, to rely on and judicially enforce, public and private arrangements in the course of securing commitments, forging partnerships and allocating responsibilities in ways that would otherwise not be open to individuals and small groups acting of their own accord. As Hart's account suggests but does not articulate, power-conferring laws, when soundly put in place, are critical means to bolster the morally

60 See further M Köpcke, *Legal Validity: The Fabric of Justice* (Oxford, Hart Publishing, 2019), especially chapter 6, section I.

61 Suarez, *De Legibus*, 5, 20, 3 and 13; 5, 21.

62 ibid 5, 25, 25.

valuable capacity for self-development that is inherent in individuals, hand in hand with placing on it restrictions warranted by fairness and respect for expectations. Suarez, unlike Hart, openly broaches the question about the moral point of these laws. His stated answer to this question leads him to nominally focus his discussion on the idea of *in*validity. But his stated answer is not the only answer that his account as a whole stands for.

CHAPTER 9

CODES AND CONSTITUTIONS (19TH ONWARDS)

The Tables are Turned

In this final segment of our historical journey, we will see the technique of legal validity definitively be projected from the domain of private law to the domain of law-making – in a sense, we will see validity appropriated by the latter domain. Legal validity is central to secular codification, both as a *subject matter* regulated by private law codes, and as the method whereby codes themselves *come into being* as pieces of law-making. But it is not codification alone that animates this turning point in our tradition. A line of scholarship frontally opposed to crafting law by statute proves to be no less decisive to the turn that legal thought will take from the early nineteenth century onwards.

This line of scholarship occupies section I of this chapter. The German Historical School of Law develops largely in reaction to the celebration of codifying statutes in the aftermath of the French Revolution and the promulgation of the Napoleonic *Code civil* (1804), France's first unitary civil code. According to Friedrich Carl von Savigny, the founder of the Historical School, a country's 'living law' is the enduring manifestation of a 'people's spirit' (*Volksgeist*). Therefore law must not – strictly speaking it cannot – have its origin in legislative fiat. Only once law has been systematised by legal doctrine, thinks Savigny, is it apt to be *restated* in enacted form. With a view to bringing German law closer to practical and doctrinal consolidation, he devotes his monumental *System des heutigen römischen Rechts* (System of Current Roman Law) (1840–9) to articulating legal rules and institutions of Roman origin that are 'still alive' in Germany.[1] Savigny's efforts not only delay Germany's jump onto the bandwagon of codification, which eventually occurs on the first day of 1900, but they also shape the understanding of private law that makes its way to the German code – and to legal systems elsewhere. Key to that understanding is the idea of a *transaction* (*Rechtsgeschäft*) and its legal validity.

The *power* to make transactions, the *power* to make valid private arrangements, is a power legally *conferred* – according to the logic of codification, not Savigny's (section II). Despite their deeply different tenets, however, Savigny's 'organic' conception of law and the codification movement share an emphasis on the law's self-regulation. And that notion European legal scholars will eventually capitalise on, prompted by a post-revolutionary aspiration to stability. Through their elaboration of the ideal of the *Rechtsstaat* or law-governed state, as section III explains, the idea of legal self-regulation matures into a focus on *legally limited law-making*, which finds its primary expression in the emerging disciplines of constitutional, administrative, and human rights law, as well as in contributions to legal theory that develop in their wake.

I. SAVIGNY ON TRANSACTIONS

Unlike Suarez and Bartolus, Savigny does not approach the subject of private transactions from the point of view of the positive *laws* governing

---

1 FC von Savigny, *System des heutigen Römischen Rechts* (Berlin: Bei Deit und Comp, 1840–9) preamble.

them. Savigny's view that law is diffusely bred in the 'people's spirit' naturally drives his focus away from positive enactments (more on this shortly).[2] He consequently fastens on the transactions themselves, and on the private relations they generate. In so doing, he draws a remarkably coherent picture of (a) *normative positions* as ingredients of these relations, the kinds of (b) *act* that effect valid changes therein, and (c) the *conditions* to which these acts are subject. They respectively concern features (i), (ii) and (iii) of legal validity highlighted in chapter 2.II. Let us consider each of them in turn.

(a) Savigny does not call *normative positions* by this name, but his account portrays individual rights (*Rechte*) as the central element of private 'legal relationships' (*Rechtsverhältnisse*). Legal relationships are the fundamental building blocks of his analysis.[3] They are the 'spiritual element of legal practice' and have an 'organic nature'.[4] A legal relationship is 'a relation from person to person, determined (*bestimmt*) by a legal rule'.[5] An individual right, in turn, is one abstractly detached side of that relationship.[6] Consistently with this, Savigny explains changes in legal relationships in terms of the generation and ending of rights, including through an alteration of persons holding them.[7] The emphasis on rights, incidentally, is not peculiar to Savigny within the German Historical School. Puchta, another prominent member of the School, structures his 1838 textbook according to the different classes of rights.[8] The modern grammar of rights has begun to bloom.

It is worth dwelling on Savigny's 'organic' understanding of a legal relationship as a relation between persons that is 'determined' by a legal rule.

---

2 At any rate the focus of his work is private law, the domain most pervaded by Roman categories (Savigny, *System*, para[graph] 1). He notes that there is barely any elaborate Roman law on the subject matter of legal sources (paras 22–7); see also chapter 4 of this book.

3 The book's substantive beginning (Savigny, *System*, para 4) presents rights as the primary reality that emerges in observing the 'state of the law' (*Rechtszustand*), immediately adding that the 'deeper foundation' (*tiefer[e] Grundlage*) of rights lies in legal relationships.

4 Savigny, *System*, para 4.

5 ibid para 53.

6 ibid para 4.

7 ibid para 104.

8 GF Puchta, *Lehrbuch der Pandekten* (Leipzig, Barth, 1838): rights over oneself, rights over things, rights over actions, rights over persons, rights over estates (*Vermögen*).

As this formulation already suggests, legal relationships and their constituent rights have a curious hybrid nature in the eyes of the Historical School. They are neither altogether creatures of legal making, nor genuinely pre-legal realities that law simply recognises. They are somewhere in between. Every legal relationship, says Savigny, consists of two elements: the 'relationship as such' (the 'tissue') and its legal determination.[9] The former is the 'material element' and the latter is the 'formal element'.[10] The material element alone is not as such legal. Indeed, several kinds of human relationship are not amenable to or in need of determination by law.[11] Friendship is not; marriage only partially. Only insofar as law 'elevates [relationships] to legal form' are they *legal* relationships involving *rights.*[12] As Puchta puts it, '[t]he existence of a right presupposes its recognition through a legal rule'.[13] Rights are not pre-legal.

And yet, Savigny tells us, the 'foundation and presupposition of all true rights', their 'germ', is a 'natural power' that is innate in individuals.[14] It is a 'power [*Macht*] over oneself and one's own strengths',[15] a 'strength inherent in each individual will'.[16] It is not clear whether by this 'power' Savigny simply means one's physical capacity to determine one's own movements, or (also) an entitlement to exercise that capacity. But he is adamant that there are no *rights* over oneself.[17] One's 'natural power' over oneself 'does not require recognition and delimitation through positive law'.[18] Rights are *over things other than oneself.*[19] Those other things may be either 'unfree nature' or 'free kindred willing beings'.[20] From this distinction Savigny derives the main branches of private law, which include the law of things (*Sachenrecht*) and the law of obligations.[21] If I have a right that you render

---

9 Savigny, *System*, para 52.
10 ibid.
11 ibid.
12 ibid.
13 Puchta, *Lehrbuch*, para 28.
14 Savigny, *System*, paras 53, 104.
15 ibid para 53.
16 ibid para 52.
17 ibid para 53.
18 ibid.
19 ibid.
20 ibid.
21 The law of obligations concerns domination over one act of another person who, for this purpose, is conceived as a 'complete' being; family law, in turn, concerns domination over another person envisaged as an 'incomplete' being (Savigny, *System*, para 53).

performance under a contract, I have 'dominion [*Herrschaft*] over one particular action' of yours.[22] Therefore, says Savigny, rights are an 'artificial extension' of the natural power we wield over ourselves.[23] They amount to 'new organs' added to our nature, whereby we can wield dominion also over the outside world.[24]

Such 'power' or 'dominion' that Savigny regards as the core of rights must not be confused with what we have been calling legal power (chapter 2). Legal power is a capacity to *change* legal rights and duties. Savigny's power is the power one enjoys *as* a right-holder, not the power to become one in the first place. Suarez had in mind the latter when *he* spoke of the 'moral power' of individuals to shape their relationships. Savigny's power, instead, is a 'space of independent domination of the individual will'[25] that accrues *once* in a relationship.

(b) But although Savigny is not nearly as enthused by the ability to bring that relationship into being as he is by the ensuing warrant for domination, his analysis of the kinds of *act* whereby legal relationships are voluntarily shaped is incomparably subtler than the equivalent one of Suarez, and probably of any earlier jurist. Suarez, as we saw in chapter 8, only understood that the individual will was somehow central to the performance of what he unstably called 'acts' or 'contracts'; it was in the field of law-making that he carefully explained the reflexive or self-referring role of the manifested will. Savigny brings that sophistication into the realm of transactions, starting with the very concept thereof.

Transactions (*Rechtsgeschäfte*) are a species of events that he jointly calls 'juristic facts' (*juristische Tatsachen*). Juristic facts are 'events that effect the beginning or the end of legal relationships'.[26] We might say: they are events that change normative positions. Such events, Savigny continues, can consist *either* in 'free actions' of the person whose legal relationships are changed, *or* in other kinds of act or event, including free actions by others. Examples of free actions of the person concerned include stealing or entering a contract. Examples of other kinds of event include being stolen from or coming of age.

22 ibid.
23 ibid.
24 ibid.
25 ibid; also paras 4, 52.
26 ibid para 104.

It is within the category of free actions of the person concerned that Savigny draws the decisive distinction by way of isolating the making of transactions from other kinds of conduct. Free actions of the person concerned differ, as he puts it, according to the way in which that person's will operates (*tätig ist*).[27] The person's will may be *either* 'immediately directed at the creation or cancellation of a legal relationship', *or* 'immediately directed at other, non-juristic purposes'.[28] In the first case, the person specifically wills the change of normative positions. In the second case, the person acts with some other goal in mind. Savigny gives a number of examples of this second scenario. They include stealing, hunting wild animals (and so acquiring them through occupation), and taking care of an absent neighbour's urgent business (and becoming entitled to claim back the expenses). None of these are transactions. Transactions correspond to the first scenario, where the person's will is 'immediately directed at the creation or cancellation of a legal relationship'. Here, Savigny explains, the will operates by being declared. And the relevant declaration of will (*Willenserklärung*) may be either unilateral (as in testamentary dispositions) or bilateral (as in contracts). The idea of a declaration of will is so central to Savigny's analysis that he sometimes calls transactions themselves 'declarations of will'.[29]

Note how this account of the technique of validity, as it is involved in transactions, comes very close to spelling out the reflexive or self-referring character of the relevant declaration of will. As we saw in chapter 2 (section II, feature (ii)), one performs a valid act, such as a transaction, by manifesting an intent to change legal positions *through that very manifestation of intent* – that is, roughly, by saying so. Savigny's falls short of making this explicit because he confusingly appeals to the 'purposes' at which the person's will is 'directed'. That appeal is confusing because, as far as the facts are concerned, even a thief may conceivably act for the purpose of changing normative positions. Homeless persons are known to commit crimes in order to become liable to spend time in jail.[30] The crucial point is not that those performing transactions act for the purpose

27 ibid.

28 ibid.

29 ibid.

30 For discussion of such examples, and the contrast with legal power, see M Köpcke, *Legal Validity: The Fabric of Justice* (Oxford, Hart Publishing, 2019) chapter 2, sections III and V. Savigny disregards this point by ruling out, too rashly, that someone preventing a neighbour's house from collapsing could 'primarily have in mind the quasi contract of *negotiorum gestio* or look up the fifth title of the third book of the Digest' (Savigny, *System*, note *g* at para 104).

of changing legal relations, but that the *means* whereby they succeed (and expect to succeed) is *by declaring that purpose*. The crucial point is that the declaration *itself* effects the normative change. The crucial point is about means, not ends. It is about the distinctive *technique* in play in the acts that Savigny helpfully portrays as yielding transactions. A declaration of will is central to a transaction precisely because it is that declaration, not the agent's purpose, that pulls off the normative feat.

(c) This generic account of the acts whereby transactions are performed is followed by a classification and discussion of the specific kinds of *precondition* to which these acts are subject. Here, too, Savigny moves from 'free actions', as the broader category, to transactions, as the narrower one. He therefore starts with the requirements of a person's general capacity to act in law (*Handlungsfähigkeit*), which include age, sound reason and requirements germane to juristic persons.[31] Then, turning to transactions, he begins by considering the necessary existence and scope of the individual will. The will's existence may be impaired by coercion and mistake,[32] and its scope may be circumscribed by self-imposed constraints in relation to condition, time or mode.[33] He next tackles formal and other requirements for the will's declaration, and discusses its possible mismatch with the underlying will.[34] To this account of preconditions common to all kinds of transactions he then adds particular discussions of certain types of transactions (such as contracts and gifts) and factors liable to affect them.[35]

Remarkably, only *after* all this does he nominally engage with the idea of legal validity. And he does so negatively, by devoting the two closing sections of his protracted discussion of juristic facts to the topic of *in*validity (*Ungültigkeit*).[36] These sections chiefly serve as a summary of the different ways in which the making of transactions can fail, can go wrong.[37]

---

31 Savigny, *System*, paras 106–13.
32 ibid paras 114–5.
33 ibid paras 116–29.
34 ibid paras 130–9.
35 ibid paras 140–201.
36 ibid paras 202–3.
37 The heading of paras 202–3 misleadingly speaks of 'Invalidity *of juristic facts*' (my emphasis). This reflects Savigny's generalising zeal. Nevertheless the discussion in those sections primarily concerns, as it should, the invalidity *of transactions*. Note that the 'invalidity' of juristic facts need not correlate to that of the relevant transaction: the 'invalidity' of a juristic fact that would otherwise end a transaction entails that the latter remains valid. Furthermore, it makes little sense to speak of '(in)valid' juristic facts outside the domain of transactions, eg in reference to thefts or earthquakes.

One may wonder why his earlier discussions are not conducted under the heading of conditions of *validity*. The reason cannot lie in a lack of taxonomic abstraction on Savigny's part (as it did in the case of classical Roman lawyers: chapter 3.I). Savigny's treatment of invalidity, like the rest of his treatise, exhibits plenty of abstraction. He comfortably draws and navigates three cross-cutting distinctions amongst *kinds* of invalidity, namely (1) complete and incomplete invalidity (nullity and voidability), (2) certain and uncertain invalidity, and (3) simultaneous and non-simultaneous invalidity.[38] Where invalidity is simultaneous, it 'is produced simultaneously with the juristic fact that thereby loses its effect'.[39] Note that this conceives of a null juristic fact as an entity that coexists in time with its own condition, ie with its own invalidity – even in German scholarship it does not get much more abstract. Savigny moreover distinguishes amongst *grounds* of simultaneous invalidity, thereby formalising the contrast that Suarez and earlier writers had more or less implicitly been working with. Simultaneous invalidity may be due *either* (i) to the lack of a necessary precondition, including personal capacity, presence of the will and compliance with the prescribed form, *or* (ii) to the transaction's prohibition by statutory enactments. The latter scenario he explains through a parallel with Roman *leges perfectae*.[40]

So his understanding of validity is sophisticated, and yet the idea primarily occupies a negative place in his work. As in the case of Suarez, Savigny's main concern is with *in*validity. Like Suarez, too, Savigny is well aware of the various formal and other requirements that an act must meet, over and above not being legally prohibited, in order to amount to a valid transaction. That he nevertheless does not portray the law as thereby *conferring* power, as *validating* our acts, must be explained chiefly by reference to two considerations. Here as well, these considerations take us back to the author's understanding of the fundamental point or role of the relevant laws in respect of the conduct they regulate. Firstly, Savigny does not regard the performance of a transaction as an exercise of *power*

38 Savigny, *System*, para 202.

39 ibid.

40 ibid para 203. Savigny endorses the *lex non dubium* presumption that legislative prohibition entails nullity (para 203) and, in an excess of venerating fervour, he even claims that Romans used a stable conceptual and terminological distinction between nullity and voidability (note *e* at para 202 and accompanying text; cf chapter 3.I of this book).

at all, innate or conferred. Secondly, and more importantly, the *law* that determines the conditions of validity, like the *law* that determines the resulting legal relationships, has a nature that is not altogether different from that of the relationships it determines. For the law that bestows on relationships 'legal form' is itself a set of rules sustained by the shared consciousness of the people – this is ultimately why those relationships are neither wholly legal nor wholly pre-legal. In the eyes of Savigny, law is not a genuinely external agent that might be said to freshly confer on us a power we would otherwise lack.

Indeed, law does not spring from an exercise of *agency* at all. Laws, unlike transactions, are not made through declarations of will. Positive law, the 'people's law' (*Volksrecht*), 'lives in the shared consciousness of a people', to the point that even the logical formulation of a legal rule involves an 'artificial process' of abstraction.[41] Law is made by the people (*das Volk*): not through the deliberate disposition (*Willkür*) of any individual member of that people, but 'invisibl[y]' through its spirit or *Volksgeist*.[42] Needless to say, Savigny is conscious of the contemporary reality of statutory law, as his extensive survey of the 'sources' (*Quellen*) of private law demonstrates.[43] But, on his account, legislation only gives 'externally recognisable existence' to law that was already present and binding.[44] Legislation primarily serves to supplement the people's law and to adjust it to changing needs where 'intentional, and thus personal intervention' is called for.[45]

It is therefore no coincidence that legislation focally comes into view at the very end of his discussion of transactions, as liable to curb, by prohibiting, what would otherwise be indefeasible legal arrangements – in the way of Roman *leges* in relation to the *ius civile*.[46] Although Savigny insists that legislation is not subordinate to the people's law as such, still

41 Savigny, *System*, paras 7, 13.

42 ibid para 7. Note that such 'real law' (para 8) is not identical with custom. Custom, for Savigny, is only the *mark* (*Kennzeichen*) of positive law, not its originating cause (*Entstehungsgrund*) (para 12).

43 Savigny, *System*, book 1 (paras 1–51).

44 ibid para 13.

45 ibid.

46 In his earlier positive discussion of the preconditions of validity, legal prohibitions come in only tangentially, primarily as a subset of 'immoral' (*unsittliche*) conditions, the emphasis being on the condition itself rather than on the law banning it: Savigny, *System*, paras 122–4.

less redundant on it, one of his comparisons is particularly revealing. He suggests that legislation, and the legal rules it enshrines, is to the underlying legal institutions (the basic rules of law) what a judicial decision is to the particular legal relationship on which it pronounces (where, we must understand, the judge is not exercising discretion).[47] In this important sense, the legal positions to which legislation gives 'recognisable existence' already existed independently of it.

The marked asymmetry we find between Savigny's conception of transactions and his conception of law-making must in one sense remind us of earlier writers we have studied – particularly Suarez, the canonists and the Romans. But unlike those writers, Savigny expressly plays up the asymmetry between transactions and laws. It is part of his battle cry. Early on in his treatise he warns against the 'confusion of concepts' involved in pursuing the analogy between contracts and legislation, an analogy he finds characteristic of the pernicious idiosyncrasy prevailing 'in recent times', particularly in France.[48] His acid attack on such 'recent' views denounces the understanding of legislation as 'the only true and genuine source of law', which relegates custom to a marginal place.[49] Hence also, he scathingly notes, 'the unconditional value attributed nowadays to comprehensive codes of law, and the luminous expectations that are bound up with their formulation'.[50]

II. CODIFYING PRIVATE LAW

But just that unconditional value and those luminous expectations very much carry the day even in Germany, as the newly founded German Empire embraces private law codification. The French economy had flourished since its 1804 code superseded patchy regional customs and regimes. In 1873, the constitution of the German Empire is changed to confer on the Empire the power centrally to legislate on private law. The result is the *BGB* (*Bürgerliches Gesetzbuch*). Its content is closely based on the body of scholarship developed by Savigny (the *Pandektenrecht*). The *BGB* prominently addresses declarations of will, their preconditions,

---

47 Savigny, *System*, para 5.
48 ibid para 6.
49 ibid para 28; also paras 29–31, 50–1.
50 ibid para 28.

and their nullity (*Nichtigkeit*), and it speaks throughout of what is valid (*gültig, geltend*) and what not.[51] But it is a code. It is law made, itself, through a valid declaration of will – on 18 August 1896, by the German Emperor upon approval by the Bundesrat and the Reichstag.[52] The legal meaning of this declaration modifies, indeed replaces, existing legal rules in private law.[53]

Quite naturally the enactment of the *Code civil* and the *BGB*, and of codes elsewhere, must at the time have been perceived, even presented, as positive law more or less overtly *conferring* on individuals a uniform set of tools to mould their relationships on equal standing across the relevant nation state. Rudolf Henle lucidly expresses this understanding in a private law monograph written a few years after the *BGB*'s promulgation.[54] Henle portrays the private legal order as 'engirding' individuals with a set of legal weapons or tools to be used at their pleasure (within limits).[55] It is a mistake, says Henle, to think of the individual will as a self-sufficient generator of legal effects, effects that the legal order is only able, negatively, to curb.[56] To be sure, he stresses, one should also stay clear of the opposite misunderstanding, the view that the legal system alone pulls the strings. We *do* exercise power in performing transactions, but it is power to operate the legal machinery, to open and close the 'watergate' of law: 'power to engage foreign power'.[57]

As I see it, Henle voices the codification-inspired move in legal thought that renders explicit what was only latent in earlier conceptions of the ability

---

51 The French *Code civil* also repeatedly refers to the '*validité*' of contracts, marriages, wills, and other transactions, and to them being (or not being) '*valables*'; the heading of Book 3, title 3, chapter 2 reads '*Des conditions essentielles pour la validité des conventions*' (On the essential conditions for the validity of agreements).

52 As it figures in the *Reichsgesetzblatt* 1896, p 195, n 21, issued on 24 August 1896.

53 On the transition, in Germany, from a usage-based to an enactment-based understanding of the binding force of laws, and the relation of this transition to the *iura novit curia* principle and the emergence of mass reproduction technology, see T Simon, 'Geltung: Der Weg von der Gewohnheit zur Positivität des Rechts' (2005) 7 *Rechtsgeschichte* 100.

54 R Henle, *Vorstellungs- und Willenstheorie in der Lehre von der juristischen Willenserklärung* (Leipzig, A Deichert'sche Verlagsbuchhandlung Nachf (Georg Böhme), 1910) 340–58.

55 Henle, *Vorstellungs- und Willenstheorie*, 356 ('*ich umgürte Dich mit diesen Waffen, gebrauche sie nach Deinem Wohlgefallen*'); the reference to the *BGB* is at 347.

56 ibid 341–2.

57 ibid 345, 356 ('*Macht ... fremde Macht anzurufen*').

to make transactions.[58] Key to this move, in turn, is an understanding of the nature of the corresponding *laws* as being in the relevant sense independent from the individuals whose acts they bear on, so that these laws may in truth bestow or confer a power the individuals in question did not already have. And the laws are thus independent, on this understanding, largely because they are themselves products of targeted exercises of agency. They are products of a technique for crafting general legal changes of potentially far-reaching scope. The technique is by no means new. But the legal culture that has grown out of the French Revolution exalts this technique and assigns it a strategic place in the scheme of legal sources. This technique is focally instantiated by legislation, of which a code is an especially ambitious form.

We must travel back to late-eighteenth-century France to appreciate the novel understanding and constitutional place of this technique.[59] France's break with its political past is given initial and lasting expression in the 1789 Declaration of the Rights of Man and of the Citizen. According to article 6 of this Declaration, '[l]aw is the expression of the general will'. The democratic technique for making law is not only a process to manufacture laws that will realise the ideals of the Revolution. It also *embodies* these ideals. Rights to political participation and to equality before a general law are therefore vindicated hand in hand with specific freedoms from state intervention. The 'general will' is ultimately the will of the 'nation', wherein all sovereignty resides per article 3. On this view, the legislature's ability to make binding laws originates in the nation, not in God as for Suarez. And that ability is genuine power exercised by the legislature as a willing agent; the legislature is not a sheer mouthpiece of an operative *Volksgeist*.

Legislative power is power to make laws that will bind the nation's members. According to the prevailing political philosophy of the day,

58 Ihering, the last prominent member of the German Historical School, is more explicit in this respect. Unlike in early Roman law, he says, where law grew out of the individuals' exercise of private violence on which the law merely placed a 'stamp', we now understand our will to be operative only given the law's prior authorisation that yields violence-free spaces (R von Ihering, *Der Geist des römischen Rechts auf den verschiedenen Stufen seiner Entwicklung*, 3rd edn (Leipzig, Vreitkopf und Härtel, 1873) 107–9).

59 For an excellent survey of some main developments outlined in this section, M Fioravanti, *Appunti di storia delle costituzioni moderne: Le libertà fondamentali* (Turin, Giappichelli, 1995).

the members of the nation figuratively confer such power on the legislature in the founding 'social contract'.[60] This conferral finds symbolic reflection in the passing of the 1789 Declaration by the French National Constituent Assembly. And it finds *legal* reflection, to some extent, in the 1791 French constitution. I say 'to some extent' because, although this constitution, like subsequent ones, is a legal document that legally regulates the exercise of legislative power, indeed that 'delegate[s]' legislative power on the relevant assembly,[61] the constitution's legal ascendancy over legislation is still rather faint. Importantly, the ascendancy does not materialise in robust mechanisms for controlling the legality of legislation. The parallel American Revolution, by contrast, is largely inspired by a distrust of legislatures and soon enough conceives of its constitution as a legally binding constraint on public power.[62] But the French Revolution is suspicious of the judiciary, which it regards as a shadow of an absolutist past. So it primarily entrusts the protection of rights to a legislature that in many respects is the supreme public institution. After all, Rousseau had said that 'the general will is always right'.[63]

To the extent that a constitution is not a *legal* limit of the legislature's ability to make law, there is less conceptual space, or less opportunity, for thinking of that ability as conferred *by law*, and for reasoning and talking about the *legal validity* of legislation. Continental legal thought does not firmly embrace this mode of reasoning and talking until well into the twentieth century, as we will soon see. But that step is nurtured by important developments in nineteenth-century legal thought.

---

60 This line of thought is most immediately represented by Rousseau's *Du Contrat Social* (1762) as well as, in a sense, Montesquieu's *De L'Esprit Des Lois* (1748); it is echoed in Sieyès influential pamphlet *Qu'est-ce que le Tiers-Etat?* (1789). But it has more longstanding roots. It reaches back, inter alia, to Locke's *The Second Treatise of Government* (1690) and Hobbes' *Leviathan* (1651). Indeed, Delacroix (*Legal Norms and Normativity: An Essay in Genealogy* (Oxford, Hart Publishing, 2008), especially 135ff) identifies 1593 as the key date for the shift, from the point of view of positive law, from a divine to a human foundation of law-making power.

61 French Constitution of 1791, Title 3, article 3. The constitution devotes Title 3, by far the longest of its seven Titles, to the allocation and exercise of 'public powers' (*pouvoirs publics*), legislative, executive and judicial, on the premise that '[t]he nation, from which alone all powers emanate, may exercise such powers only by delegation' (Title 3, article 2).

62 *Marbury v Madison*, 5 U.S. 137 (1803) ('an act of the Legislature repugnant to the Constitution is void').

63 Rousseau, *Du Contrat Social*, Book 2, chapter 3.

Some of these developments we have already touched on. They bear little connection, on their face, to the idea of a binding constitution.[64]

III. THE *RECHTSSTAAT*

The developments I have in mind arise in the context of a post-revolutionary aspiration to stability. As against the revolutionary commendation of path-breaking *acts of will*, the emphasis is now – particularly in German legal culture, but not only there – on the liberties to be enjoyed under the *impersonal* rule of an increasingly robust *Rechtsstaat*, a state governed by law. The *Rechtsstaat* is regarded as a more natural guarantor of rights than the sheer say-so of particular legislatures or of self-proclaimed constituent bodies. It is easy to see how Savigny's voice contributes to shaping this climate, not least through his alternative conception of the nation – *das Volk* – as a continuing historical reality not identical with or liable to be represented by the members of a specific generation purporting to make legal *tabula rasa*.

But nineteenth-century European legal thought does not deny, not as vehemently as Savigny, that law is the result of the say-so of individuals and institutions. Private law codification is a clear indication of this. Rather, the ideal of the *Rechtsstaat* manifested in landmark texts of this time is the ideal of a legal say-so that is not steered by extra-legal, 'political' concerns, but that occurs *within* a self-contained legal system, a system with its own internal, so far forth *purely legal*, rationale. It is telling, for instance, that the *Code civil* devotes its opening section to settling matters of constitutional status. It starts by proclaiming that '[l]aws are executory throughout the whole French territory, by virtue of the promulgation thereof made by the first consul',[65] and goes on to specify a chorus of provisions that ensure the hierarchical pre-eminence and effective application of the laws

64 Other developments are more closely related to that idea. In nineteenth-century Germany, as Jansen shows, the question whether royal decrees are legally subordinated to the early constitutions of German states involves an incipient form of juristic concern with the legal validity of norms, and is probably associated with the emergence of '*Geltung*' as a technical concept: see N Jansen, *Rechtswissenschaft und Rechtssystem: Sieben Thesen nur Positivierung des Rechts und zur Differenzierung von Recht und Rechtswissenschaft*, Würzburger Vorträge zur Rechtsphilosophie, Rechtstheorie und Rechtssoziologie, vol 56 (Baden-Baden, Nomos Verlag, 2018) theses 4 and 5 (33–45).

65 *Code civil*, article 1.

thus promulgated (including the binding force of 'police laws', a ban on judicial legislation and *non liquet*, and the subjection of private agreements to laws on public order).[66] In so doing, the code, as it were, projects the systematicity internal to private law onto the very arrangement of legal sources within the state. An act of legislation speaks to the institutional position of legislative law-making. It is law that concerns itself. It is law that does not appeal to a higher-order legitimating source, legal or moral, but implicitly affirms the self-vindicating, self-regulating, self-referring nature of the legal system.

Parallel developments are palpable in another area of legal scholarship that flourishes at that time: administrative law, or public law more generally. Ancient forms of executive power tainted by hereditary privilege and corruption have given way, on the prevailing post-revolutionary understanding, to a rational, *because law-governed*, public administration, complex enough to need, and organised enough to sustain, a dedicated body of legal rules and doctrines – and in due course, a dedicated jurisdiction. Scholars of this booming public law, including Otto Mayer and Georg Jellinek, treat the state, perhaps for the first time, as an object of *juristic* analysis. In various ways they grapple with the puzzle that the state creates the very law that governs the state. Mayer sees in the notion of an administrative act, whereby a legally regulated administration makes binding determinations for particular cases, the culmination of the ideal of the *Rechtsstaat*.[67] Jellinek takes on a broader constitutionalist perspective. 'State power', he writes, 'is governing power that cannot be derived from any further source, that is, governing power arising from itself.'[68] Jellinek also stresses the difference between evaluative, goal-oriented studies of the state, germane to the science of 'politics', and the kind of descriptive-explanatory analysis he regards himself as unfolding.[69] In the same book, *General Theory of the State*, he portrays law as a set of *norms*, primarily characterised by their *validity* (*Gültigkeit*).[70] The book, his magnum opus, appears in 1900, the same year that Germany's *BGB* comes into force.

---

66 *Code civil*, articles 3–6.

67 O Mayer, *Deutsches Verwaltungsrecht*, vol I (Leipzig, Verlag von Duncker & Humblot, 1895) paragraph 5 (53–66); see also paragraph 8 (94–104). Mayer's pioneering elaboration of German administrative law is deeply inspired in French doctrine.

68 G Jellinek, *Allgemeine Staatslehre*, 3rd edn (Berlin, Häring, 1914) 489 ('*Staatsgewalt ist … nicht weiter ableitbare Herrschergewalt, Herrschergewalt aus eigener Macht*').

69 ibid 6ff.

70 ibid 332–3.

Consider for a moment the perspective of someone who begins to study law at that time, especially in German-speaking Europe. One will be exposed to a discipline marked by a heightened degree of self-consciousness, manifested in technical reasoning premised on a rich conceptual cosmos of the law's own making, in both private and public law. One will be witness to an all-round intellectual enthusiasm for a mode of acting-in-the-law no longer chiefly confined, as for many centuries, to the private domain, but increasingly acknowledged, in some ways *replicated*, in the domain of acts performed by official institutions of countless kinds. For, indeed, analogies between the private and the public domain, even at that time, extend beyond particular administrative doctrines being framed on the model of private law ones. The very *Code civil* states that contracts 'are binding as laws' (*tiennent lieu de loi*) on those who made them.[71] The analogy between contracts and legislation, so despised by Savigny, is capitalised on by both jurists and philosophers. Jellinek goes as far as to say that public law is the very foundation of private law, as the latter allows individuals to set in motion the state's power.[72] In short, as a student of law one will be taught a technique for bringing about legal effects at scales large and small, effects bankable in a distinctly legal currency. And one will understand that the way to bring them about is to act within the framework of an authorising law, a law that is ultimately self-authorising.

Hans Kelsen is one of these students. He reads law at the University of Vienna, where Jellinek has taught.[73] In a sense, what Henle is to Savigny in respect of private transactions, Kelsen is to Suarez, Savigny and other nineteenth-century European thinkers, in respect of law-making acts. Central to Kelsen's work is the exceptionless claim that acts make law only insofar as they occur within a legally empowering or authorising framework. This is true of legislative acts as well, indeed of constitutional enactments: they, too, are what they are, as a matter of law, by reference to the system's presupposed 'basic norm'. In so arguing, Kelsen extends and generalises the logic of the *Rechtsstaat*, the logic underlying the systematisations of private

---

71 *Code civil*, article 1134 (now 1103) (*Les conventions légalement formées tiennent lieu de loi à ceux qui les ont faites*).

72 Jellinek, *Allgemeine Staatslehre*, 385.

73 On the respects in which the early Kelsen openly distances himself from Jellinek, see S Paulson, 'Hans Kelsen's Earliest Legal Theory: Critical Constructivism' in SL Paulson and B Litschewski-Paulson (eds), *Normativity and Norms: Critical Perspectives on Kelsenian Themes* (Oxford, Clarendon Press, 1998) 26–32.

and administrative law, in comprehensively accounting for the entire legal order: all the way from its constitution to judicial pronouncements and private transactions, which he presents as hierarchically ordained in various ways.[74] The common metric that runs through this hierarchy is *legal validity*, and the basic unit to which the metric applies is the *legal norm*. Even private transactions are legal norms.[75] What legal science for almost two millennia had treated as a domain of study in its own right is now explained on the model of law-making. And not chiefly on the model of law-making *acts*, but of the *product* of such acts, a product duly detached from its originating context and contemplated as an impersonal, objective, more or less free-standing entity, apt to figure in juristic reasoning: the legal norm. The science of law is now a science of norms.

Every regime we have surveyed in this book was self-regulating to some extent, and acknowledged as such by juristic thought. But at the juncture we are presently considering, juristic thought acclaims and perhaps perfects law's self-regulating character, for reasons related to underlying social and political transformations. But those reasons lie beyond Kelsen's jurisprudential concerns. Kelsen's legal theory is committed to methodological 'purity'. There is no room in his account for questions of justice or questions relevant to empirical social science. As a result, Kelsen largely gives voice to the *law's* self-understanding. He largely acts as a spokesman for the law's internal logic, which he is fascinated by. 'A plant is unable to tell the classifying botanist anything about itself',[76] he notes, but law and the classifying legal theorist stand in a different relation. Kelsen's theory very helpfully verbalises certain fundamental assumptions of ordinary legal reasoning.[77] He also takes his spokesmanship to well-known

---

74 On the earlier, in some ways comparable, integrating and abstracting current known as American 'classical legal thought', influential in the United States between 1865 and 1940, D Kennedy, *The Rise and Fall of American Legal Thought* (Washington, Beard Books, 2006).

75 Or, more accurately, they create legal norms: H Kelsen, *General Theory of Law and State*, A Wedberg (tr) (New York, Russell, 1945) 136–42; H Kelsen, *The Pure Theory of Law*, 2nd edn, M Knight (tr) (Berkeley, University of California Press, 1967) 256–62. Hart approvingly echoes Kelsen's view that private powers can be usefully understood as 'limited legislative powers' in the hands of individuals (HLA Hart, *The Concept of Law*, 2nd edn (Oxford, Clarendon Press, 1994) 96). There are parallels with Bentham's claim that every exercise of legal power is a participation in the sovereign's 'power of imperation' (J Bentham, *Of Laws in General*, HLA Hart (ed) (London, The Athlone Press, 1970) chs 2 and 9).

76 Kelsen, *The Pure Theory of Law*, 6.

77 See Köpcke, *Legal Validity*, 8–9.

extremes. Such is, for instance, his view that '[t]he legal order cannot have any gaps'.[78] Or his claim that, legally speaking, there is no 'absolute nullity' as 'everything to which the law refers becomes law'.[79] Or his suggestion that legal empowerments implicitly authorise the making of unlawful final decisions.[80] Kelsen's law controls even its own lack of control. It truly is nobody's fool.

Quite apart from the inherent appeal of this ingenious portrait of law for an expanding legal science, Kelsen's account is attractive in the way it endeavours to combine law's character as a self-regulating system of *norms* with the norms' origin in and standing exposure to human *acts*. Although, in Kelsen, this latter facet is largely subordinate to the former, the interplay between the two facets marks some particularly suggestive (and problematic) tenets of his work.[81] A positive legal norm is the product, the meaning, of an act of will.[82] A legal system can therefore be regarded *either* ('statically') as a set of norms, *or* ('dynamically') as a set of norm-producing acts.[83] And, seeing as the system's 'efficacy' is a precondition of its existence, coups d'état and other constitutional overthrows *interrupt* the sequence of validation that would otherwise connect earlier to later (amended) constitutions of the same state. It follows that the present legal system's ultimate positive source, what he calls the 'historically first' constitution, may have just come into force during yesterday's coup.[84] In so arguing, Kelsen's work offers to reconcile the reality that the constitutional and so legal shape of states is subservient to political transformations, a reality vividly experienced by late nineteenth- and early twentieth-century Europeans (not least Austrians), *with* the understanding that once such

78 Kelsen, *General Theory of Law and State*, 147.

79 ibid 161. For a discussion of this claim in the context of the problem of 'unconstitutionality' of legislation, see P Yowell, 'The Negative Legislator: On Kelsen's Idea of a Constitutional Court' in M Belov (ed), *Courts and Politics* (New York, Routledge, forthcoming).

80 Kelsen, *General Theory of Law and State*, 153ff; Kelsen, *The Pure Theory of Law*, 267ff.

81 In the latest phase of Kelsen's work, the second facet acquires such pre-eminence that it leads to the collapse of central tenets of his account, even to his admission of the possibility of normative conflicts (H Kelsen, *General Theory of Norms*, M Hartney (tr) (Oxford, Clarendon Press, 1991) 123ff, 211ff), and to his abandonment of the doctrine the 'basic norm' (for this norm 'is not the meaning of an act of will': H Kelsen and others, 'Diskussionen' (1963) 13 *Österreichische Zeitschrift für öffentliches Recht* 117, 119).

82 Kelsen, *The Pure Theory of Law*, 2ff.

83 ibid 70–1.

84 Kelsen, *General Theory of Law and State*, 115–9.

changes are made, and until they are unmade, a self-contained and logically consistent system of norms can be presupposed to exist on their back, and *is* so presupposed by anyone reasoning in the law. A legal system, as it were, can be *both* an impersonal *Rechtsstaat*, *and* something made, put there, by discrete individuals at more or less defined historical moments.

Kelsen's combination of these two broad understandings of law furnishes an attractive repository of ideas to nurture a legal culture that, especially in the aftermath of WWII, is concerned with preserving the heritage of the *Rechtsstaat* compatibly with re-founding legal orders on the strength of fresh decisions and commitments, national and supranational. Key amongst such decisions and commitments are constitutional documents now devised and, echoing American doctrines, hailed as embodying legally binding constraints on legislative power. These constraints are primarily articulated in the language of rights ('human rights', 'fundamental rights', etc).[85] Kelsen's legal theory – but not only his – reworks a grammar that is very much in demand across the Western world. It is the grammar of legal validity, but focused on the *legal validity of norms*. It is a grammar for conceiving of a legal system as deliberately self-limiting, and so, amongst other things, of constitutionalised rights as constraints, *embraced by law*, on the law-maker's legal power. Moreover, Kelsen's account – like others – supplies these ideas wrapped in a purportedly value-neutral theoretical apparatus, palatable to those wary of pernicious ideological appropriations of legal science in the recent past.

Judicial assessment of legislation and other exercises of public power in light of legally enshrined moral standards, and the legal consequences of that assessment, become a focal point of legal and political argument, and also, directly or indirectly, of influential strands of legal theory, by no means limited to a narrowly understood Kelsenian school. In England,

---

85 Remarkably, neither the framers of the US Constitution contemplated, nor Kelsen himself supported, a justiciable bills of rights: for discussion, see P Yowell, *Constitutional Rights and Constitutional Design: Moral and Empirical Reasoning in Judicial Review* (Oxford, Hart Publishing, 2018) 148ff. Kelsen's stance is articulated in H Kelsen, 'Wesen und Entwicklung der Staatsgerichtsbarkeit' in H Triepel, H Kelsen, M Layer and E von Hippel, *Wesen und Entwicklung der Staatsgerichtsbarkeit: Überprüfung von Verwaltungsakten durch die ordentlichen Gerichte*, Veröffentlichungen der Vereininung der deutschen Staatsrechtslehrer, vol 5 (Berlin and Leipzig, Walter de Gruyter, 1929) 30–85; an English translation is available in L Vinx (ed), *The Guardian of the Constitution: Hans Kelsen and Carl Schmitt on the Limits of Constitutional Law* (Cambridge, Cambridge University Press, 2015) chapter 1.

Austin's conception of law-as-command (1832)[86] gives way, within just over a century, to Hart's emphasis (loosely foreshadowed by Bentham) on legal empowerment and 'secondary rules', rules presented, in their union with 'primary rules', as the 'key to the science of jurisprudence'.[87] In England and elsewhere, in the field of legal theory it is very much an age of rules about rules, of reasons about reasons, of interpretations about interpretations, of agreement about (dis)agreement – even of theory about theory. It is also an age of legal validity, although of validity conceived primarily as it implicitly figures in the reasoning of judges seeking to establish the considerations – criteria – for discriminating amongst putative rules. In one of its more extended forms, a judge-centred legal theory, sometimes denounced for excessively replicating its own object of study, routinely casts central problems in terms of *criteria of legal validity*, and the objects to which these criteria apply as *legally valid rules or norms*.

Validity thereby gains specialised *theoretical* currency as a property of legal norms, in the context of a legal culture that is grappling with the place of constitutions, legislation and rights perhaps more self-consciously than ever before. But the *legal technique* to which this body of literature somewhat opaquely refers is not privy to the areas of law that focally deal with the making and review of general legal standards, notably constitutional law. In fact, legal practice and argument in this area probably invoke the label 'validity' much less assiduously ('constitutionality' is often preferred) than they do in many other areas, including in private, procedural or administrative law, where the things of which validity is predicated are much more transparently *acts*, such as transactions, licences or resolutions, or even various kinds of representations or proofs thereof, many of them as familiar to ordinary citizens as to lawyers.

Today, technology multiplies the frequency, sophistication and speed of our interactions with strangers; and, partly as a consequence, public administration (itself of a changing nature) is called on to interact with us in countless new domains of life, such as professional training, welfare provision, immigration, tax, employment safety or industrial control. Thus the grammar of legal validity becomes all the more essential as an all-purpose tag and technique to bring coherence into a fabric of deeply

[86] J Austin, *The Province of Jurisprudence Determined*, WE Rumble (ed), Cambridge Texts in the History of Political Thought (Cambridge, Cambridge University Press, 1995).

[87] Hart, *The Concept of Law*, 81.

diverse legal relationships – public and private, local and international, fleeting and lasting, digital and analogue. Such relationships have the potential to realise justice because moulded in a technique that largely brackets away questions about justice.[88] It is a technique that makes central a datable manifestation of intent, whereby, subject to constraints of substance and form, individuals and institutions can shape the normative landscape. It is a technique as old as European legal culture, but newly refined and more firmly understood. It is a technique fit to craft the future for years to come.

---

88 For an argument, see Köpcke, *Legal Validity*.

CHAPTER 10
CONCLUSION

I. TAKING STOCK

There is much that the history of legal validity can teach us. It can help us understand not only the nature of this technique, but also its point and manifold uses.

These findings emerge from what in one sense is the story of the propagation of a term. We may briefly recap this story.

Inchoate uses of the term are manifest as Roman legal thought devises strategies, especially in the hands of praetors, to give legal clothing to the creation, change and reversal of private arrangements beyond the rigid structures of the received *ius civile*. An incipient grammar of non-technical words, mostly invoking degrees of unfitness or impropriety not stably distinguished from the notion of prohibition, serve legal thought's need to track the status of these acts against the backdrop of the complex interplay between, amongst other things, the jurisdictions of civil and praetorian law.

Medieval canonists in turn capitalise on a more streamlined grammar of legal validity in organising a haphazard body of provisions into the legal system of the ever-growing Church. Gratian's pioneering harmonisation, as refined in a subsequent Gloss, envisages transactions and certain procedural acts as being *either* valid *or* invalid, a status now understood to be independent of the idea of prohibition. The first official Church codification captures this binary status through variations in the term-family '*valere*', including the adjective '*validum*' (valid), the adverb '*valide*' (validly), and the noun '*validitas*' (validity), which remain the primary linguistic forms of our present 'validity' palette. Occasional extension of this language to official resolutions, even to law-making acts, foreshadows the continuous predication of 'validity' *across* private and public law that later centuries will generalise in the secular domain.

Stirrings of this generalisation are already patent as the Middle Ages draw to a close. Bartolus recurrently appeals to 'validity' both in pondering the status of transactions in light of different territorial jurisdictions, and in pondering the status of these jurisdictions themselves. Subsequent elaborations of the European *ius commune* home in on the notion of the validity of transactions. Whereas Suarez draws a sophisticated picture of the governing *laws*, Savigny focuses on the valid *acts* whereby transactions are performed. Savigny, however, denies that law itself could be the product of a valid act of will, woven as law is, in his view, into the 'organic' reality of rights and legal relationships. Ironically, it is very much in the name of rights that deliberately promulgated enactments will eventually be conceived as sources of, and standards for, the legal validity of norms.

But there's no magic in a word. This book's claim that a uniform *technique* gradually unfolds over the centuries, transiting from private to public law, must be vindicated by pointing to deeper similarities between the forms of legal reasoning evinced in the juristic works of each period. Chapter 2 laid out six main features of the technique of legal validity, as it operates in legal systems today. Throughout our historical journey we have witnessed these features arise, combine and develop.

The first feature (i) picks up the *result* of valid acts. Valid acts change normative positions, that is, they change the rights, duties and powers that certain persons have in law. The second feature (ii) concerns the *way* in which valid acts change normative positions, namely by the agent saying so. Both these features are palpable from Roman times, notably in the field of transactions. Suarez in the seventeenth century offers an elaborate rendition of the second feature in the domain of law-making, in terms of a self-referring expression of the ruler's intent. In a no less elaborate manner, Savigny in the nineteenth century accounts for this feature in the domain of private law, by describing a transaction's 'declaration of will'.

That valid declarations of will are inherently subject to *conditions* (feature (iii)) is a premise that classical Roman law capitalises on by invoking prohibitive statutes (*leges imperfectae, minus quam perfectae* and *perfectae*) and otherwise providing procedural remedies to curb or alter the status of transactions. Medieval canon law has an even more differentiated concern with formal and substantive limits on transactions. Medieval canon lawyers, too, hold that a prohibition may invalidate a transaction, but their understanding of the notion of prohibition is sharper than the Roman one: prohibition is now closely associated with the ideas of wrongfulness and sin. Bartolus, Suarez and Savigny, in turn, all work with a robust distinction between formal and substantive validity criteria of transactions. Only with codification and constitutionalism is the distinction projected onto law-making acts as well, and applied to their abstracted products – rules or norms.

But who or what sets conditions of validity? The *system* in light of which something is valid (feature (iv)) receives disparate characterisations over time. The unstably dual regulation in Roman law, wherein prohibitive *leges* make provisions over and above the *ius civile* standard, gives way to a uniform regime within the canon jurisdiction. But, in the secular domain, Bartolus again must wrestle with criteria of validity determined by both city statutes and Roman law. His reconciliation of city statutes with the Roman governing framework foreshadows the coherently *legal* understanding of a unified order celebrated in the age of codification and constitutionalism. That age leaves behind Suarez's troubling conception of the law-maker as empowered by God, and Savigny's denial that validity conditions can be ultimately set by legislated law.

Transactions that meet conditions of validity can in principle have effects beyond the time and place of their creation, and in this sense *circulate* (feature (v)), even in classical Roman law. However, the circulation of Roman transactions is hampered both by the unsettled relationship between the *ius civile* and the *ius honorarium*, and by the general preclusion of the institutions of cession of rights, agency and contracts in favour of third parties. The binary logic of validity and invalidity refined by canon lawyers facilitates more secure reliance on transactions and sacramental arrangements. Bartolus can even contemplate whether transactions are valid outside their originating territorial jurisdiction. And both Suarez and Savigny, like present-day jurists, take for granted that transactions can circulate in numerous further ways as a matter of law.

With variations in emphasis, therefore, the sequence of historical snapshots we have looked through in this book reflects an overall consistent, broadly parallel build-up of the five key features of the technique of validity. So it is not surprising that the *language* of validity, feature (vi), itself ripens and spreads at a matching pace. This genealogical account helps confirm that the six features do indeed hang together, that the name 'validity' tracks a distinct legal technique, forming an association that has withstood the test of time.

II. VALIDITY'S POWER

This historical evolution of legal validity is allegorically represented in the image on page xiii. The image separately traces the *parcours* of validity in the domain of private law and in the domain of law-making. It relies on the rough distinction between the validity of transactions and the validity of enactments, and illustrates the respective prominence of these ideas in juristic thought over time. The image helps to bring out what is perhaps the most striking mark of the development charted in this book: validity's long incubation in the private law domain and its relatively recent extension to the domain of public law and law-making, an extension that in some areas of legal argument amounts to a pre-eminent concentration on valid enactments (specifically rules or norms) at the expense of valid transactions, titles, and other procedures or institutions of law.

This curious fact about the evolution of validity is accompanied, as we have noticed at several points in the book, by a riddling shift in how legal thought conceives of the power to make private transactions. For centuries, positive laws regulating transactions were said to *curb* or *restrict* a power held by individuals quite independently of those laws. The idea that such laws *confer* power is a relatively recent one. Hart popularises the view of laws governing transactions as 'power-conferring rules', rules that 'provide individuals with facilities for realising their wishes'.[1] This view is also reflected in doctrinal writings at the dawn of the codification era. For Suarez, by contrast, laws that set conditions of validity 'remove or impede' a 'power' that 'the human will has by natural law'.[2] This is why he calls them 'invalidating laws' (*leges irritantes*).

We are now in a position to relate these two developments – the extension of the logic of validity to the domain of law-making, and the shift towards a view of private law regimes as power-*conferring* rather than power-*restricting*. Considered in isolation, the latter shift, the shift in the conception of private power, might be taken to denote a shift in the content of private law rules over time. Earlier phases of our legal culture, it might be felt, deployed private law chiefly to repress and rein in the scope of free individual action, whereas more recent regimes open up newer and better possibilities of autonomous action and relationship. We have moved, it might seem, from constraining to enabling law. Although there is doubtless some truth in this proposition, it must not eclipse the important correlation that exists between a period's conception of private power (as restricted or conferred) and that same period's conception of law-making. The shifting emphasis from restriction to conferral of private power, I suggest, reflects not so much a change in the *content* of private law rules as a more fundamental shift in the understanding *of positive law itself.*

Take the Roman case. Classical Roman law develops strategies to make and unmake private transactions, by way of overcoming the rigidities of the *ius civile*. The general point of these strategies is not to cramp voluntary arrangements – it is very much to facilitate them. And yet the strategies in question are commonly cast by jurists in terms of the curbing, breaking or rescission of transactions. Why? The answer follows from the nature of these strategies themselves. Their central operation is through procedural remedies, granted by praetors. Such remedies characteristically come in after the fact and in a context of litigious contestation. What is more, the bodies of law wherein these strategies are introduced (praetorian law, prohibitive *leges*) are largely regarded as ancillary to the focally customary *ius civile* baseline – which they supplement but cannot supplant. Formally at least, these new bodies of law must presuppose and build upon

1 HLA Hart, *The Concept of Law*, 2nd edn (Oxford, Clarendon Press, 1994) 27.
2 F de Suarez, *Tractatus De Legibus ac Deo Legislatore*, 5, 25, 25.

any powers and abilities individuals already wield *iure civili*. And it is that new law that focuses juristic discussion on point, the discussion that becomes the chief record and testimony of classical Roman law.

Canon lawyers, too, are interested in facilitating rather than obstructing the recognition and circulation of valid transactions. They even insist that some transactions can be prohibited and *nevertheless* legally valid. But the acts and arrangements in question include sacraments, which positive laws can hardly be regarded, in canon law, as freshly conferring the power to celebrate, seeing as this power has a divine foundation. And while it is not sacraments that Suarez specifically has in mind when *he* speaks of legal transactions, his account similarly portrays the human legislator as in the relevant sense empowered by God. Positive laws cannot be an ultimate source of legal power, in Suarez's account, because the source of whatever power they *themselves* have is pre-legal: hence also why he does not separate the validity of laws from their justice. And yet these are the same positive laws that Suarez elsewhere describes as enabling widespread reliance on and judicial enforcement of private arrangements, and as creating public offices and roles.

In Savigny, finally, we come across a catalogue of validity conditions that even more closely tracks, indeed inspires, those of present-day legal orders. Many such validity conditions go to ensure that the subject performing the transaction gives expression to his free, informed, uncoerced will. But again Savigny does not portray such positive law as *conferring* on people the power to make transactions. For positive law itself emanates from the 'spirit' of the very people whose transactions are at stake – the *Volksgeist*.

I have left out Bartolus. It might be thought that he is a counterexample to the trend I am identifying. But in fact he confirms it. Unlike the previous writers, Bartolus *does* have room to cast some city statutes as enabling rather than disabling (as 'permissive' rather than 'prohibitive'). City statutes enable the performance of transactions, he says, when they either relax the conditions set by Roman law or create altogether new forms of official disposition. But then, in Bartolus' account, city statutes are legally valid themselves. Their validity stands on the robustly legal footing provided by the Roman framework. This *avant-la-lettre* constitutionalist claim is an early precedent and foundation of the view of law, now familiar to us, as essentially self-validating: that is, as not deriving its legal validity from anything pre-legal, such as the nation, natural reason or God. It is in the context of this view that modern codes, and private law regimes more generally, are portrayed as *conferring* on individuals *legal* power, a power these individuals would not otherwise hold.

An important lesson to be learned from this is that the contrast between restriction and conferral of legal power is liable to be overstated, and is therefore potentially misleading.[3] As I foreshadowed in chapter 2, and have explained elsewhere at greater length,[4] sound criteria of validity confer power hand in hand with limiting its exercise. Strictly speaking, there can hardly be such thing as legally unlimited legal power. Properly used, the technique of validity serves to *allocate* the responsibility to decide to those who ought to bear it, and correspondingly to circumscribe the decision-making capacity of others. Validity can be a key instrument to foster reasonable self-direction, and thus justice in community, precisely because it enables us to assign competencies, delegate choices and otherwise *delimit* the scope of justified action in the course of undertaking commitments, designing ventures and forging lasting relationships that go to shape our identity as individuals and groups. This general point and potential of legal validity has not essentially changed over the centuries.

What is more: the fact that validity was introduced in the past for purposes that we can relate to in the present, albeit in social and political settings very different from our own, should encourage us to explore the potential of this technique to handle legal transformations we may face in the *future*. It is probably fair to say that the present theoretical purchase of the notion of validity is largely owed to accounts of the legal order of nation states. These accounts presuppose and elaborate a sharp distinction between the lay and the official world, which in its demarcated constitutional roles has the final legal say on the life of a community implicitly or explicitly understood to occupy a circumscribed territory in a world divided into sovereign states. Questions about validity, in such accounts, centrally supply the test for membership of rules in the state legal order, a test officially set and administered. Legal validity is focally a creature of the constitutional state.

---

3 In a similar spirit, see the defense of 'positive' over 'negative' constitutionalism in NW Barber, *The Principles of Constitutionalism* (Oxford, Oxford University Press, 2018).

4 See M Köpcke, *Legal Validity: The Fabric of Justice* (Oxford, Hart Publishing, 2019), especially chapters 4–7.

But it is no less true, and historically more accurate, to say that the constitutional state is a creature of legal validity. Writing at the juncture at which territorially bound jurisdictions begin to consolidate within what formally remains a single Empire, Bartolus resorts to the logic of validity to legally vindicate the political independence of the emerging polities. '*Civitas sibi princeps*' (the city is its own emperor) projects the Emperor's law-making power at a micro level, by reproducing multiple instances thereof, coexisting side by side. But the slogan is *itself* a legal proposition, advanced under the auspices of Roman law and subject to what qualifications Roman rules may yield. That state sovereignty is compatible with legal limits on state power, indeed that sovereignty cannot reasonably amount to unlimited jurisdiction, is an important truth that the development of supranational regimes in recent decades may be helping legal thought to regain consciousness of.[5] We are not juristically orphaned in making sense of that reality. Roman, medieval and early modern jurists were very much in the business of weaving fabrics of rules that transcended existing jurisdictions without absorbing them.

So when legal thought today is faced with binding human rights covenants, non-state practices spoken of and heeded as law, projects of supranational 'integration', or virtual forms of agency and community, it does well to look beyond the resources of theoretical writings that take as their default canvas a political and constitutional environment that plays down as residual what deserves urgent attention. But shifting canvas need not involve shifting tools. In searching beyond the resources of state-focused theories, legal thought must not close its eyes to an age-old and continually oiled legal toolkit that is central to many of the above novel ventures, a toolkit whose capacities and dangers, resources and pitfalls, were carefully pondered by generations of jurists well before the spread of state-centric legal reasoning.

Being an architectural element present in both civil and common law jurisdictions, the technique of validity is decisive, for example, to prospects and methods of *harmonisation* of European private law regimes – while, at the same time, it lies at the core of the *individuation* of member states,

5 For a helpful articulation of this truth, see T Endicott, 'The Logic of Freedom and Power' in S Besson and J Tasioulas (eds), *The Philosophy of International Law* (Oxford, Oxford University Press, 2010).

in a turn of legal thought that curiously mirrors the one at the origins of statehood. Validity provides a common grammar wherein to cast claims otherwise hard to commensurate in the face of ideological diversity and clashing views about justice. Even the Church's legal order was built on a foundational *contrast* between invalidity and sin, between what is null and what is wrongful, a contrast that entails that valid choices can be identified independently of their moral merits. Validity's use in channelling interaction across cultural, linguistic and national boundaries may still be in its infancy. In a sense, valid digital objects such as currencies, codes, signatures or certificates are a consolidating further stage in the evolution of validity's toolset, perhaps approaching the ultimate form of circulation of valid choices beyond their originating scene.

Just as Bartolus once decoupled Roman *law* from the Roman *Emperor*, thereby paving the way for the emergence of distinct countries on the back of a shared Roman heritage, perhaps it is now time to decouple legal validity from the broader state apparatus we have grown to narrowly associate validity with. That association is belied by nearly two millennia of legal history.

BIBLIOGRAPHY

Austin, J, *The Province of Jurisprudence Determined*, WE Rumble (ed), Cambridge Texts in the History of Political Thought (Cambridge, Cambridge University Press, 1995)

Barber, NW, *The Principles of Constitutionalism* (Oxford, Oxford University Press, 2018)

Bartolus, *Bartoli interpretum iuris civilis coryphaei, In duodecim libros Codicis, commentaria* (Basel, Froben, 1562)

—— *Bartoli interpretum juris civilis coryphaei, In jus universum civile, commentaria* (Basel, Froben, 1562)

—— 'Tractatus de Tyrannia' in Bartolus, *Consilia, Quaestiones et Tractatus* (Venice, 1585)

Bellomo, M, *The Common Legal Past of Europe: 1000–1800*, LG Cochrane (tr), Studies in Medieval and Early Modern Canon Law, vol 4 (Washington DC, The Catholic University of America Press, 1995)

Bentham, J, *Of Laws in General*, HLA Hart (ed) (London, The Athlone Press, 1970)

Black, J, 'Constitutional ambitions, legal realities and the Florentine state' in WJ Connell and A Zorzi (eds), *Florentine Tuscany: Structures and Practices of Power* (Cambridge, Cambridge University Press, 2000)

Boosfeld, K, 'Die beiden Statutenlehren: Geschichte eines rechtshistorischen Missverständnisses' (2019) 136 *Zeitschrift der Savigny-Stiftung für Rechtsgeschichte: Germanistische Abteilung* 76

Brie, S, *Die Lehre vom Gewohnheitsrecht: Eine historisch-dogmatische Untersuchung, Erster Teil: Geschichtliche Grundlegung* (Breslau, von M & H Marcus, 1899)

Buckland, WW, *A Text-Book of Roman Law from Augustus to Justinian* (Cambridge, Cambridge University Press, 1921)

Canning, J, *The Political Thought of Baldus de Ubaldis* (Cambridge, Cambridge University Press, 1987)

Christensen, K, 'Introduction' in A Thompson, J Gordley and K Christensen, *Gratian: The Treatise on Laws with the Ordinary Gloss*, Studies in Medieval and Early Modern Canon Law, vol 2 (Washington, The Catholic University of America Press, 1993)

Cicero, *De Domo Sua Ad Pontifices Oratio*, RG Nisbet (ed) (Oxford, Oxford University Press, 1939)

—— 'In Verrem' in Cicero, *Orationes*, vol III, W Peterson (ed) (Oxford, Oxford University Press, 1963)

—— 'Philippicae' in Cicero, *Orationes*, vol II, AC Clark (ed) (Oxford, Oxford University Press, 1963)

—— *De Legibus Libri Tres*, English version in JEG Zetzel (ed), *On the Commonwealth and on the Laws* (Cambridge, Cambridge University Press, 1999)

—— *De Re Publica*, English version in JEG Zetzel (ed), *On the Commonwealth and on the Laws* (Cambridge, Cambridge University Press, 1999)

Delacroix, S, *Legal Norms and Normativity: An Essay in Genealogy* (Oxford, Hart Publishing, 2008)

Delgado Echeverría, J, 'Las leges irritantes en De Legibus de Francisco Suárez como normas de competencia' (2006) 29 *DOXA Cuadernos de Filosofía del Derecho* 405

Di Paola, S, *Contributi ad una Teoria della Invalidità e della Inefficacia in Diritto Romano* (Varese, Multa Paucis, 1966)

Duve, T, 'Von der Europäischen Rechtsgeschichte zu einer Rechtsgeschichte Europas in globalhistorischer Perspektive' (2012) 20 *Rechtsgeschichte* 18

Endicott, T, 'The Logic of Freedom and Power' in S Besson and J Tasioulas (eds), *The Philosophy of International Law* (Oxford, Oxford University Press, 2010)

Finnis, J, 'Aquinas on *jus* and Hart on Rights' (2002) 64 *Review of Politics* 407

—— *Natural Law and Natural Rights*, 2nd edn (Oxford, Oxford University Press, 2011)

Fioravanti, M, *Appunti di storia delle costituzioni moderne: Le libertà fondamentali* (Turin, Giappichelli, 1995)

Fögen, MT and Teubner, G, 'Rechtstransfer' (2005) 7 *Rechtsgeschichte* 38

Gaius, *Institutes*, Latin/English version in EA Whittuck (ed) and E Poste (tr), *Gai Institutiones or Institutes of Roman Law by Gaius* (Oxford, Clarendon Press, 1904)

Gratian, *Decretum Gratiani* (*Concordia Discordantium Canonum*) (Rome, in aedibus Populi Romani, 1584)

Grotius, H, *De Iure Belli ac Pacis Libri Tres. In quibus ius naturae & Gentium: item iuris publici praecipua explicantur* (Paris, Nicolas Buon, 1625)

Hart, HLA, *Essays on Bentham: Jurisprudence and Political Theory* (Oxford, Clarendon Press, 1982)

—— *The Concept of Law*, 2nd edn (Oxford, Clarendon Press, 1994)

Henle, R, *Vorstellungs- und Willenstheorie in der Lehre von der juristischen Willenserklärung* (Leipzig, A Deichert'sche Verlagsbuchhandlung Nachf (Georg Böhme), 1910)

Hobbes, T, *Leviathan*, JCA Gaskin (ed) (Oxford, Oxford University Press, 2008)

Iglesias, J, *Derecho Romano: Instituciones de Derecho Privado*, 6th edn (Barcelona, Ariel, 1972)

Ihering, R von, *Der Geist des römischen Rechts auf den verschiedenen Stufen seiner Entwicklung*, 3rd edn (Leipzig, Vreitkopf und Härtel, 1873)

Jansen, N, '*Ius commune* (Gemeines Recht)' in J Basedow, KJ Hopt and R Zimmermann (eds), *Handwörterbuch des Europäischen Privatrechts* (Tübingen, Mohr Siebeck, 2009)

—— 'Testamentary Formalities in Early Modern Europe' in KGC Reid, MJ de Waal and R Zimmermann (eds), *Comparative Succession Law*, vol I: Testamentary Formalities (Oxford, Oxford University Press, 2011)

—— *Rechtswissenschaft und Rechtssystem: Sieben Thesen nur Positivierung des Rechts und zur Differenzierung von Recht und Rechtswissenschaft*, Würzburger Vorträge zur Rechtsphilosophie, Rechtstheorie und Rechtssoziologie, vol 56 (Baden-Baden, Nomos Verlag, 2018)

Jellinek, G, *Allgemeine Staatslehre*, 3rd edn (Berlin, Häring, 1914)

Justinian, *Digest*, Latin/English version in T Mommsen, P Krüger and A Watson (eds), *The Digest of Justinian* (Philadelphia, University of Pennsylvania Press, 1985)

—— *Institutes*, Latin/English version in JT Abdy and B Walker (eds), *The Institutes of Justinian* (Cambridge, Cambridge University Press, 1876)

—— *Code*, English translation in SP Scott (ed), *The Civil Law*, vols 12–15 (Cincinnati, The Central Trust Company, 1932)

Karlowa, O, *Der Römische Civilprozess zur Zeit der Legisactionen* (Berlin, Weidmannsche Buchhandlung, 1872)

—— *Römische Rechtsgeschichte I* (Leipzig, Veit und Comp, 1885)

Kaser, M, *Das Römische Privatrecht I: Das Altrömische, das Vorklassische und Klassische Recht* (Munich, C.H. Beck'sche Verlagsbuchhandlung, 1955)

—— *Römische Rechtsgeschichte*, 2nd edn (Göttingen, Vandenhoeck & Ruprecht, 1967)

—— *Über Verbotsgesetze und Verbotswidrige Geschäfte im Römischen Recht* (Vienna, Verlag der Österreichischen Akademie der Wissenschaften, 1977)

Kelsen, H, 'Wesen und Entwicklung der Staatsgerichtsbarkeit' in H Triepel, H Kelsen, M Layer and E von Hippel, *Wesen und Entwicklung der Staatsgerichtsbarkeit: Überprüfung von Verwaltungsakten durch die ordentlichen Gerichte*, Veröffentlichungen der Vereininung der deutschen Staatsrechtslehrer, vol 5 (Berlin and Leipzig, Walter de Gruyter, 1929)

—— *General Theory of Law and State*, A Wedberg (tr) (New York, Russell, 1945)

—— *The Pure Theory of Law*, 2nd edn, M Knight (tr) (Berkeley, University of California Press, 1967)

—— *General Theory of Norms*, M Hartney (tr) (Oxford, Clarendon Press, 1991)

Kelsen, H and others, 'Diskussionen' (1963) 13 *Österreichische Zeitschrift für öffentliches Recht* 117

Kennedy, D, *The Rise and Fall of American Legal Thought* (Washington, Beard Books, 2006)

Keogh, A, 'The Codification of Canon Law' (1928) 10 *Journal of Comparative Legislation and International Law*, 3rd Series, 14

Köpcke, M, *Legal Validity: The Fabric of Justice* (Oxford, Hart Publishing, 2019)

Landau, P, 'Gratian and the *Decretum Gratiani*' in W Hartmann and K Pennington (eds), *The History of Medieval Canon Law in the Classical Period, 1140–1234: From Gratian to the Decretals of Pope Gregory IX* (Washington, The Catholic University of America Press, 2008)

Livius, *The History of Rome (Ab Urbe Condita Libri): The First Eight Books*, D Spillan (ed) (London, Henry G Bohn, 1853)
Locke, J, *The Second Treatise of Government*, TP Peardon (ed) (New York, The Liberal Arts Press, 1952)
Mayer, O, *Deutsches Verwaltungsrecht*, vol I (Leipzig, Verlag von Duncker & Humblot, 1895)
Meier, E, *Die Rechtsbildung in Staat und Kirche* (Berlin, Georg Reimer, 1861)
Mommsen, T, *Römisches Staatsrecht*, vol III, part I (Leipzig, Hirzel, 1887)
—— *Römisches Staatsrecht*, vol III, part II (Leipzig, Hirzel, 1888)
Montesquieu, *De L'Esprit des lois*, vols I and II, L Versini (ed) (Paris, Gallimard, 1995)
Padoa-Schioppa, A, *A History of Law in Europe: From the Early Middle Ages to the Twentieth Century* (Cambridge, Cambridge University Press, 2017)
Paulson, S, 'Hans Kelsen's Earliest Legal Theory: Critical Constructivism' in SL Paulson and B Litschewski-Paulson (eds), *Normativity and Norms: Critical Perspectives on Kelsenian Themes* (Oxford, Clarendon Press, 1998)
Pope Gregory IX, *Decretales* (Venice, Apud Iuntas, 1615)
Puchta, GF, *Lehrbuch der Pandekten* (Leipzig, Barth, 1838)
—— *Cursus der Institutionen*, vol I (Leipzig, Breitkopf und Härtel, 1841)
Rousseau, JJ, *Du Contrat Social ou Principes du Droit Politique*, B Bernardi (ed) (Paris, Flammarion, 2001)
Savigny, FC von, *System des heutigen Römischen Rechts* (Berlin, Bei Deit und Comp, 1840–9)
Schulte, JF, *Die Geschichte der Quellen und Literatur des Canonischen Rechts von Gratian bis auf die Gegenwart*, vol I (Stuttgart, Ferdinand Enke, 1875)
—— *Die Geschichte der Quellen und Literatur des Canonischen Rechts von Gratian bis auf die Gegenwart*, vol II (Stuttgart, Ferdinand Enke, 1877)
Sieyès, EJ, *Qu'est-ce que le Tiers-État?*, R Zapperi (ed) (Geneva, Droz, 1970)
Simon, T, 'Geltung: Der Weg von der Gewohnheit zur Positivität des Rechts' (2005) 7 *Rechtsgeschichte* 100
Skinner, Q, *The Foundations of Modern Political Thought*, vol I: *The Renaissance* (Cambridge, Cambridge University Press, 1997)
Smith, JAC, 'Bartolo on the Conflict of Laws' (1970) 14 *American Journal of Legal History* 157, 247
Suarez, F de, *Tractatus De Legibus ac Deo Legislatore*, Latin/Spanish version in F de Suarez, *Tratado de las Leyes y de Dios Legislador* (Madrid, Instituto de Estudios Políticos, 1967)
Tasioulas, J, 'Justice, Equality, and Rights' in R Crisp (ed), *The Oxford Handbook of the History of Ethics* (Oxford, Oxford University Press, 2013)
Thompson, A, Gordley, J and Christensen, K, *Gratian: The Treatise on Laws with the Ordinary Gloss*, Studies in Medieval and Early Modern Canon Law, vol 2 (Washington, The Catholic University of America Press, 1993)
Tierney, B, *Religion, Law, and the Growth of Constitutional Thought 1150–1650* (Cambridge, Cambridge University Press, 1982)

Ullmann, W, *Jurisprudence in the Middle Ages* (London, Variorum Reprints, 1980)
—— *Principles of Government and Politics in the Middle Ages* (New York, Routledge, 2010)
Ulpian, *Rules*, Latin/English version in JT Abdy and B Walker (eds), *The Commentaries of Gaius and the Rules of Ulpian*, 3rd edn (Cambridge, Cambridge University Press, 1885)
Vinx, L (ed), *The Guardian of the Constitution: Hans Kelsen and Carl Schmitt on the Limits of Constitutional Law* (Cambridge, Cambridge University Press, 2015)
Waldron, J, *Law and Disagreement* (Oxford, Oxford University Press, 1999)
Willems, PGH, *Droit Public Romain ou Les Institutions Politiques de Rome depuis l'Origin de a Ville jusqu'a Justinian*, 5th edn (Louvain, Peeters, 1833)
Winroth, A, *The Making of Gratian's* Decretum, Cambridge Studies in Medieval Life and Thought, 4th Series (Cambridge, Cambridge University Press, 2004)
Woolf, CNS, *Bartolus of Sassoferrato: His Position of Medieval Political Thought* (Cambridge, Cambridge University Press, 1913)
Yowell, P, 'The Negative Legislator: On Kelsen's Idea of a Constitutional Court' in M Belov (ed), *Courts and Politics* (New York, Routledge, forthcoming)
—— *Constitutional Rights and Constitutional Design: Moral and Empirical Reasoning in Judicial Review* (Oxford, Hart Publishing, 2018)
Zimmermann, R, *The Law of Obligations: Roman Foundations of the Civilian Tradition* (Cape Town, Juta & Co Ltd, 1990)

INDEX

ABOUT THE AUTHOR

Maris Köpcke is a Research Fellow at the Faculty of Law, University of Oxford, and a Lecturer at the Faculty of Law, University of Barcelona. She was previously a Fellow and Tutor in Law at Worcester College Oxford. She holds a doctorate from Oxford, which won the European Award for Legal Theory 2011, and LL.M. degrees from the European Academy of Legal Theory and Harvard Law School. Her research focuses on a range of problems in legal and constitutional theory and she is the author of *Legal Validity: The Fabric of Justice* (Hart Publishing, 2019).

www.ingramcontent.com/pod-product-compliance
Ingram Content Group UK Ltd.
Pitfield, Milton Keynes, MK11 3LW, UK
UKHW021825120926
8556IPUK00043B/1032

9 781780 688152